THE CHURCH AND REVOLUTION IN NICARAGUA

THE CHURCH AND REVOLUTION
IN NICARAGUA

Laura Nuzzi O'Shaughnessy
&
Luis H. Serra

Ohio University Center for International Studies
Latin America Studies Program

Monographs in International Studies
Latin America Series Number 11

Athens, Ohio 1986

Library of Congress Cataloging-in-Publication Data

O'Shaughnessy, Laura Nuzzi.
    The church and revolution in Nicaragua.

    (Monographs in international studies. Latin America
series ; no. 11)
    Bibliography: p.
    1. Catholic Church--Nicaragua--History--20th century.
2. Church and state--Nicaragua--History--20th century.
3. Nicaragua--Church history. 4. Nicaragua--Politics
and government--1979-   . I. Serra, Luis H.
II. Title. III. Series.
BX1442.2.084 1986   322'.1'097285   85-26923
ISBN 0-89680-126-8

ISBN 0-89680-126-8

CONTENTS

One of the most controversial phenomena in Nicaragua following the Sandinista victory of July 1979, was the role, or, more accurately, the "roles" played by the Catholic church. While some of the clergy, especially at the parish level, viewed the revolution as an historic opportunity to implement the "preferential option for the poor" bravely proclaimed by Latin America's bishops at Medellín Colombia in 1968, the bulk of the hierarchy led by Archbishop Miguel Obandó y Bravo quickly recoiled from, and became highly critical of, the new system. This conservative reaction came in spite of the fact that the Sandinistas issued statements guaranteeing freedom of religion, explicitly rejected the Marxist argument that "religion is the opiate of the people," named priests to important positions in government, encouraged and promoted religious celebrations, and put "In God we trust" on newly-minted coins (above the revolutionary slogan "Free Fatherland or Death" on the flip side of the image of Augusto C. Sandino).

By June of 1984, tensions between the government and most of the church hierarchy had escalated to the point that the government was formally accusing certain segments of the church of being directly involved in a counterrevolutionary "internal front" organized in coordination with the CIA's surrogate "contra" (counterrevolutionary) war against Nicaragua. Though the Archbishop immediately denied these charges, the subsequent airing of security force video and sound tapes of a clandestine conversation between a priest and a contra leader left little doubt that at least a segment of the church was, by that time, deeply involved in subversive activities.[1] Significantly, the terrorist tactics discussed in that conversation were remarkably similar to some to be found in a subsequently-exposed manual for guerrilla warfare which had been prepared by the CIA and distributed to contra leaders earlier that year.[2] In August, suspicions that Catholic clergy were actively involved in counterrevolutionary activities were again reinforced by the publication in the U.S. media of excerpts from an internal memo by John J. Meehan, an executive of W. R. Grace & Co., which describes a meeting between Archbishop Obando and U.S. business executives in New York earlier that year. On that occasion Obando reportedly discussed "a 'development plan' to thwart

the Marxist-Leninist policies of the Sandinistas,"
including the training of anti-Sandinista leaders, and
bragged that "his campaign represented the best
organized opposition in Nicaragua to the Sandinista
efforts to install a Marxist-Leninist society."[3]

Throughout the first four years of the Reagan
Administration most of the U.S. mass media took the
side of Nicaragua's conservative anti-Sandinista
Catholic hierarchy. Obando was usually depicted as a
valiant and progressive leader who had "ardently[4]
supported the Sandinistas during the insurrection"
and had only gradually become a critic of the "left-
ist" regime as he subsequently became aware of its
abusive, "communistic" nature. This vision of the
Church-State conflict was simply incorrect. Though
opposed to Somoza, Obando and much of the hierarchy
had __never__ supported the Frente Sandinista de
Liberacion Nacional (FSLN). Indeed they had frequently cooperated in efforts to block the Sandinista rise
to power. Almost immediately after the victory it was
apparent to scholars in the field that the potential
for a serious schism within the church as well as for
conflict[5] between church and state was clearly
present.

In this volume, Laura N. O'Shaughnessy and Luis
H. Serra examine and analyze the growing division
within the church and between church and state in the
first several years of the Sandinista revolution.
Both authors have done considerable fieldwork in
Nicaragua. Professor O'Shaughnessy was a member of an
interdenominational lay mission team that travelled to
Central America in 1981 to observe the role of the
churches in that region. Fascinated by the drama
unfolding within the Nicaraguan church, she returned
to do research on various occasions thereafter. Luis
Serra, an Argentine scholar educated in Argentina and
in the United States, left a doctoral program in the
United States to work in popular education in Nicaragua soon after the Sandinista victory. In the ensuing
half decade he was involved in grassroots education
and mobilization, first as part of the 1980 literacy
crusade, and later as an employee of the Ecumenical
Center for Agrarian Education and Promotion (CEPA),
the Ministry of Housing and, finally, the National
Union of [Small] Cattlemen and Ranchers (UNAG).

Generally sympathetic to the goals of the
Sandinista revolution and to that segment of the
Catholic Church which has followed the "preferential
option for the poor," O'Shaughnessy and Serra offer
similar, though by no means identical, analyses.
O'Shaughnessy examines the political role of the
Church from the period of the insurrection through the

visit of Pope John Paul II in March of 1983. She contends that the lack of unity in the Church's posture toward the revolution can generally be attributed to 1) the ambiguity of church doctrine as reflected in the pronouncements of the Vatican and in the documents emerging from the Latin American Bishops' conferences of Medellin, Colombia (1968) and, especially, Puebla, Mexico (1979); 2) differing class orientations (clergy having direct daily contact with the poor masses seemed more prone to adopt a prorevolutionary stance, whereas members of the hierarchy with more frequent contact with the minority privileged classes tended to be more conservative); and 3) perceived institutional interests (the hierarchy felt that the revolution and what they labeled the "popular church" were a threat to their authority and traditional patterns of control while progressive clergy saw involvement in the revolution as the only way for the church to adapt to a rapidly changing world).

Luis Serra, on the other hand, sees the unfolding conflict as a fully predictable product and component of ideological struggle. Prior to the revolution, the elitist system of control had propagated its ideology and values (fatalism, capitalism, anti-communism, competitive individualism, consumerism, racism and sexism) through four major institutions: the family, the school, the mass media, and the church. Since the first three were relatively weak, the church had played a major role in transmitting the values of the dominant class. After the FSLN victory, the government passed laws and implemented policies which had a major impact on the family, the school system, and the mass media. A more autonomous institution, the church was much less changed by government policy. Therefore Serra feels that it is not surprising that it became a principal vehicle for the propagation of pre- or counter-revolutionary ideas. Of course as a former employee of CEPA, Serra does not ignore the positive role of the progressive clergy. However, he feels that in a hierarchical, almost medieval, institution such as the church, what really counts is the behavior of the top leadership.

The situation described and analyzed by O'Shaughnessy and Serra has important implications which extend far beyond the borders of Nicaragua. For scholars who have been researching the different forms of religiosity in Latin American societies and the changing influence models used by the church in the 20th Century,[6] the Nicaraguan experience may prove a testing ground for theories generated elsewhere. For all of us, Nicaragua to date and in the future may provide partial answers to important questions such as: Is church-state conflict inevitable at the outset of a social revolution? Can the church keep up with and adapt to the process of rapid socio-political change taking place in Latin America?

Thomas W. Walker
Athens, Ohio

PART 1
THE CONFLICTS OF CLASS AND WORLDVIEW:
THEOLOGY IN REVOLUTIONARY NICARAGUA

Laura Nuzzi O'Shaughnessy

BACKGROUND

Unlike the Cuban and the Mexican revolutions, the Nicaraguan revolution was the first in Latin America to be made with the active participation of Christians from both Catholic and Protestant churches. While a majority of the Christian laity and clergy supported the revolution from the start of the insurrection against Anastasio Somoza, the Catholic hierarchy moved cautiously from a position of criticism of the Somoza government to tentative support for the legitimacy of armed insurrection under certain circumstances.

After the triumph of the Sandinista Front on July 19, 1979, one of the first acts of revolutionary celebration was the presentation of a mass led by Archbishop Miguel Obando y Bravo. Despite these cordial beginnings, the relations between the church hierarchy and the Nicaraguan government soon began to deteriorate. By the summer of 1983, Archbishop Obando had become one of the principal opponents of the Sandinista regime. The Episcopal conference of Nicaragua's Catholic bishops, while publicly maintaining a facade of unity with the Archbishop, was in fact deeply divided, as was the Catholic laity. Unfortunately, the well-publicized papal visit of Pope John Paul II served not to heal these divisions but to aggravate them. Why such discord emerged within the Nicaraguan Christian community is the subject of this essay.

There are two explanations for the polarization of the Nicaraguan Catholic Church and the friction between the church and the Nicaraguan government. One lies in the ambivalence of Catholic social teaching. Within the Nicaraguan context, different priorities in the reconstruction process can be similarly legitimated by Catholic social teaching, especially by reference to the concluding documents of the Latin American Bishops Conferences which took place at Medellín, Colombia, in 1968 and Puebla, Mexico, in

1

1979. Therefore Catholic social doctrine cannot be employed as the ultimate authority to decide which interpretation[1] of the revolutionary process is the "correct" one. This problem of doctrine is greatly compounded by the second explanatory factor; the economic and political divisions which have emerged largely, although not exclusively, along class lines, in support of or opposition to the Nicaraguan government.

Those who lost economic and political power after the revolution went into opposition to the government and endorsed a doctrinally traditional and politically reformist vision of the church and society they would like to see. Those who gained power with the success of the Sandinista Front for National Liberation (FSLN) embraced the transformational liberated vision of Christianity and the sociopolitical restructuring of Nicaraguan society which offers them participation in the revolutionary process.

In this study, we examine the complex relationship between religion and class in Nicaragua from 1978 through the visit of Pope John Paul II in March 1983. Throughout this work, an attempt has been made to let the Nicaraguan bishops speak for themselves, especially through their letters.

We begin with a brief overview of the contrasts between the documents of the Latin American Bishops Conferences of Medellín and Puebla and how they inform Christian action in Nicaragua. Next we discuss the origins of the divisions between the Nicaraguan government and the church hierarchy, which are symbolized most visibly by the continued participation of five priests in government. As this conflict simmered from May 1980 to the present, the Catholic hierarchy began increasingly to voice the complaints of those who are in opposition to the revolution. Outright criticism of the government surfaced in February 1982 with the publication of a bishops' letter criticizing the government's relocation of the Misquito Indians. At several critical junctures the Vatican intervened in the Nicaraguan process. Yet its role also has been inconclusive because of the divisions within the Vatican itself over politics and doctrine.

THE SOCIAL TEACHING OF THE LATIN AMERICAN CATHOLIC CHURCH

The transformations of Vatican II, 1962-1965, informed the Latin American Bishops Conference (CELAM) which met at Medellín and set the tone for a Christian social analysis grounded in the search for human dignity.[2] To this end, the 1968 conference produced

Med.

2

the strongest document in defense of the poor and the immediacy of their plight ever issued by Catholic bishops. The Latin American bishops analyzed the actual conditions of their continent and offered a causal analysis for these conditions when they spoke of the tension between classes in relation to internal and external colonialism and of the institutionalized violence of the social structure.

The bishops called for the creation of a just social order and stated that the responsibility for this task rested with the bishops themselves as well as with the laity, which must "develop their own grass-roots organization for the redress and consolidation of their rights and the search for true justice."[3] It is important to remember, in anticipation of future criticism of the "people's church," that the Christian base communities, or comunidades eclesiales de base (CEBs) as they are frequently called, evolved from the Medellín conference with the encouragement of the bishops.

In addition to advocating the development of basic Christian communities to aid in the transformation of society, the bishops called for concientizacíon (consciousness raising) in the light of the gospels. They argued that before a social transformation could take place, a Christian social awareness must be developed:

> The uniqueness of the Christian message does not so much consist in the affirmation of the necessity for structural change, as it does in the insistence on the conversion of men which will in turn bring about this change. We will not have a new continent without new reformed structures, but above all, there will be no new continent without new men, who know how to be truly free and responsible according to the light of the Gospel.[4]

Many contradictory analyses have been written about the Latin American Bishops Conference which took place in Puebla, Mexico, 1979.[5] To understand the role of Christianity in Nicaragua, we must ask whether the Puebla documents can be considered a continuation of the commitment to social justice initiated with the Medellín conference.

In my opinion, the Puebla conference was initially designed to weaken the commitment that was taken at Medellín. Under the direction of conservative Catholic bishops and theologians, the original draft documents for this conference returned the church's teaching to its pre-Medellín, pre-Vatican II

3

position with its emphasis on a harmonious view of society, its defense of the common good which took precedence over partisan interests, and its criticism of the CEBs and of liberation theology. However, the final Puebla documents do not constitute a complete retrenchment from the position taken at Medellín. Because the unexpected deaths of two popes (Paul VI and John Paul I) delayed the start of the conference, progressive Latin American theologians took the opportunity to organize themselves for action.

It is significant that at Puebla, in contrast to Medellín, important progressive Latin American bishops and theologians were in the minority. The progressive theologians had to organize themselves into a "second Puebla" and become advisors to bishops who were delegates to the conference. Thus, even though these progressives were not delegates to the conference, they were able to deflect the strength of the traditional message that was clear in the original working documents of Puebla.[6]

The final documents were ambiguous because they reflected the influence of both traditional Catholic teaching and some of the concepts of Medellín. For example, in the Puebla document, the preferential option for the poor was still important, but not exclusive, because the church must maintain its "ministry of unity" to all classes. This notion of the ministry of unity was reminiscent of the precedence of the "common good" and also minimized the reality of class conflict which had been evident in the Medellín documents. Most importantly, the need for a preferential commitment to the poor was diminished.[7]

While the Medellín documents, in many instances, were analytical and causal in nature, the Puebla documents were descriptive and inconclusive. For example, the Medellín documents interrelated their discussions of institutionalized violence and injustice; they are both lodged in the structures of Latin America:

> In many instances Latin America finds itself faced with a situation of injustice that can be called institutionalized violence, when, because of a structural deficiency of industry and agriculture, of national and international economy, of cultural and political life, 'whole towns lack necessities, live in such dependence as hinders all initiative and responsibility as well as every possibility for cultural promotion and participation in social and political life,' thus violating

4

fundamental rights. This situation demands
all-embracing, courageous, urgent and
profoundly renovating transformations. We
should not be surprised, therefore, that
the 'temptation to violence' is surfacing
in Latin America. One should not abuse the
patience of a people that for years has
borne a situation that would not be accept-
able to anyone with any degree of awareness
of human rights.[8]

The Puebla document attempted to build upon the
Medellín concepts of institutionalized violence and
injustice.

In recent years we have also seen deterioration in the political sphere. Much harm
has been done to the participation of
citizens in the conduct of their own
affairs and destiny. We also frequently
see a rise in what can be called institutionalized injustice (Med: P:16). And by
employing violent means, extremist political groups provoke new waves of repression
against segments of the common people.[9]

The Puebla document obscured the institutional nature
of injustice in the preceding statement. The responsibility for violence was placed upon extremist
political groups.
   The end result of the Puebla conference was to
open the Latin American Church once again to the
doctrinal ambiguity characteristic of traditional
Catholic social teaching and thus to lend support to
both progressive and conservative forces within the
church. Puebla in its totality -- that is, the
preliminary document and Pope John Paul II's opening
address, in which he obliquely criticized liberation
theology and a political role for the church -- was an
initial attempt to neutralize the activism initiated
after Medellín. Puebla in its documents crystallized
the divisions within the church over which direction,
traditional or prophetic, the church should follow.
   The problem for Catholic doctrine is that while
it is timeless and transcendental, to make the doctrine meaningful in either a personal or collective
sense it must be related to our lives and to the
historical period in which we live. Once this happens
(and this process began in the Catholic Church with
Vatican II), the doctrine loses part of the sense of
timelessness and of neutrality that traditional church
leaders would like it to maintain. The universality
of the social teaching cannot maintain its

abstractness when it is applied to concrete situations in given historical periods.

In a very real (empirical) sense, the conflict over Catholic social teaching unfolded in Latin America and especially in Nicaragua. What happened was that those Christians who supported the revolution took the Medellín Conference, basic Christian communities (CEBs) and concientización through the Gospels as their points of reference. Those who were opposed to the revolution argued that the Puebla documents presented a more "balanced" view of the church's overall role. To these people the correct doctrine was that which traced its roots to mainline, traditional European Catholic teaching. They argued that because the church is a universal transnational actor, it must remain "nonpartisan" and "free" to criticize injustices in all types of political systems. In actuality, those who made reference to the universality of the church's doctrine were the upper-middle classes who increasingly (and lamentably) used this tradition for political purposes.

For example, most Christians are familiar with and accept the Biblical distinction between the kingdom of heaven and the kingdom on earth. In Nicaragua, upper-middle class Catholics who did not value the collective aspects of Christianity and who emphasized the spiritual, personal quality of Christianity used this Biblical distinction to deny the connections between the kingdom of heaven and the kingdom on earth. They argued that the kingdom on earth can never be the kingdom of God. They are two separate, distinct kingdoms, and one finds salvation and liberation only in the kingdom of God. To speak of liberation on this earth is inaccurate and presumptuous since liberation belongs only to God. Liberation must be achieved by the individual's working out his/her own spiritual relationship with God. In this interpretation one finds a criticism of the audacity of liberation theology and also a doctrinal basis for nonparticipation in the preferential work for the poor. Poverty is spiritualized. One finds liberation in the next world, the transcendental world where "there is neither Jew nor Greek, there is neither slave nor free, there is neither male nor female, for you are all one in Christ Jesus."[10]

It is significant to realize that when the Latin American bishops wrote at Medellín about the transformed society for which they wanted to work in Latin America, they anticipated criticism of this vision of society, "which even now is able to give some foreshadowing of the new age." They felt compelled to state that they were not confusing temporal progress and the Kingdom of Christ. Relying on Gaudium et Spes

6

from Vatican II, they argued that temporal progress, "to the extent that it can contribute to the better ordering of human society, is of vital concern to the Kingdom of God."[11]

CHURCH-STATE CONFLICT IN NICARAGUA

Pre-Revolutionary Origins: 1978-1979

The origins of the divisions between the Nicaraguan bishops and Sandinista leadership could be seen in the pre-1979 period when the CEBs were organizing for social action and the Nicaraguan bishops were advocating a gradual change but not a violent one. What united the hierarchy and the base of the church was their anti-Somoza sentiment. While large segments of the base of the Church became pro-Sandinista the episcopate did not. The bishops never endorsed the FSLN and never definitively endorsed the need for revolution. The dominant tone of the episcopal letters written in the year preceding the Sandinista victory was Thomistic and reflected the influence of European philosophy in Catholic doctrine. Five themes were prominent in the bishops' letters: 1) they were highly critical of the level of violence in the country; 2) they abhorred the abuses of authority, which they clearly blamed on the Somoza regime; 3) they placed greater emphasis on reform of institutions as a political solution than on structural transformation; 4) they hesitated to condone violence as a solution; and 5) they never directly criticized the National Guard as an institution.

For example, in a letter of August 1978, in criticism of the Somoza regime, the bishops called for a health campaign, for better public administration (an end to corruption and incompetence in public officials), and for more prudent control of the national economy and the federal budget. Finally, the bishops called for the end of "a violent repression that has created a climate of terrifying insecurity in the citizenry but justifies itself by a supposed defense of national security."[12]

Within the same directive to the faithful, the bishops also reaffirmed the Catholic and Thomistic message of the church in that the church "continues the work of Christ, who came to preach and fulfill the kingdom of God, the kingdom of peace and justice, of love and truth, of sanctity and grace . . . . To fight for justice, peace, the development and defense of the rights of man is not making partisan politics, but instead working for that which is fundamental for the common good."[13]   In establishing this position, the

7

Nicaraguan bishops specifically informed the faithful that the position that they had taken was congruent with that of the 1971 Synod of Bishops.

The Nicaraguan bishops were somewhat ambivalent about the political solutions the Christian should endorse because their main contention was that a truly Christian solution is above partisan politics. At times they appeared to obliquely endorse the need for structural change called for at Medellín. Yet while Medellín called for the transformation of social structures based upon the re-education of the Christian conscience, the Nicaraguan bishops stated: "The originality of the Christian message doesn't directly consist in the affirmation of the necessity for structural changes [emphasis mine] but instead in the insistence on the conversion of man"[14]

When the bishops spoke of the "new socioeconomic order" they wanted to see in Nicaragua they adhered to the position the Catholic church has taken since Vatican II; the bishops defended all human rights and declined to set priorities in terms of economic, social, and political rights.[15] Thus, they asked for improvements in nutrition, health, education, housing, work, agriculture, salaries, and individual rights. They also called for the closing of the gap between rich and poor and the lessening of the foreign debt.

However, as they proceeded to specify which political rights they endorsed, their political preferences appeared more liberal-reformist in content. Significantly, in listing this political bill of rights, the bishops first assumed that they were expressing their solidarity with the popular outcry. From the bishops' perspective, the Nicaraguan people wanted:

- The authentic exercise of the right of political association, unionization, and the free election of authorities.
- The guarantee of a judiciary, independent of political power, which gives just recourse to its citizens.
- The suppression of laws which violate the liberty of expression of persons and institutions.

The episcopal hierarchy never clearly endorsed the Sandinista revolution, and neither did it acknowledge the fact that armed struggle in Nicaragua was justified. The bishops consistently argued that they could not condone violence and made reference to Pope John XXIII: "It is certain that there are situations whose injustice cries out to heaven. The temptation to resist fighting against such grave injuries of human dignity with violence is great when entire populations lacking basic necessities live in such dependence that all initiative and responsibility is thwarted, as well as all possibility of cultural promotion and participation in social and political life."[16]

As the revolution proceeded and Christian compromise seemed unattainable, the bishops cautiously moved toward a tentative acknowledgement of the necessity of violence. They warned: "Peace without justice is a dream. It may also be a dream to detain the violence of those who, tired of yielding to other means, demand justice."[17] By July 7, 1979, twelve days before the FSLN victory, the bishops issued an appeal for national nonpartisan unity based upon the Christian commitment to peace. In a reference to the Medellín documents, they stated that they had been "urging radical changes in the structures of political and social life" but today they saw that "reason has collapsed and that the established system has not responded to the incessant demands of its citizens. It would seem as though one has no choice but to kill, annihilate, even to disregard the just rule of war."[18]

While the seeds of discord between the Sandinistas and the hierarchy can be explained by the bishops' lack of endorsement of the revolution and the moderate "liberal" nature of their political solutions, the bishops' position regarding the National Guard was an anathema to the FSLN. To the Sandinistas, the Guard was despised and genocidal; it was impossible to separate the guardsmen from the Somoza regime. The bishops, on the other hand, never directly criticized the National Guard as an institution. In one letter, they warned the men who were fighting that they would have to "account for their warlike actions because the future depends on their current actions."[19] In another letter, the bishops called for a reorganization of the National Guard "on the basis of the national interest. This reorganization would not be done on the basis of either personal ties or party affiliations and the National Guard would then receive a much smaller percentage of the national budget."[20]

To the FSLN this solution, regardless of who presented it, was totally unacceptable. It must be remembered that during the American sponsored efforts at a moderate political solution to the Nicaraguan revolution in June and July of 1979, the United States, too, proposed that the National Guard be retained and integrated with the FSLN forces. Both American policymakers and the Nicaraguan bishops were interested in a reform of the Somoza system, a moderate change which would improve upon the pluralism of the past but not radically alter the future. Among

9

the Nicaraguan moderates solicited by the United
States to be part of these negotiations as late as
July 17, 1979, was Nicaraguan Archbishop Miguel Obando
y Bravo. With Obando in Caracas, Venezuela, for this
last-ditch attempt were Violeta Chamorro, widow of
slain journalist Pedro Joaquín Chamorro; industrialist
Alfonso Robelo, and leader of the Social Christian
Party, José Esteben González. Several Sandinistas who
later came to hold cabinet rank met with Archbishop
Obando before his departure to convince him not to
participate in these negotiations. Obando was asked
whether, if he could not bring himself to support the
FSLN, he would consider maintaining a position of
neutrality.[21] Because the military victory of the
FSLN was imminent, serious negotiations did not
succeed.

While the Sandinistas had reasons to distrust
the Nicaraguan hierarchy, the bishops for their part
were also wary of the Revolutionary program, its
ideology, and its broad base of support. The emerging ideology of Sandinismo was potentially threatening
to the Nicaraguan hierarchy. Sandinismo, with its
strong appeals to Nicaraguan nationalism, its uncompromising resistance to the National Guard and American imperialism, captured the imagination and
conviction of many Nicaraguans. On an affective and
symbolic level it could challenge Christianity. The
church anticipated a struggle for the hearts and minds
of the faithful and feared that Sandino could replace
Christ as liberator.

Unfortunately, these apprehensions were given
credibility by the Sandinistas' enthusiastic reference
to Sandino with imagery that had theretofore been
reserved for Christ. When the Sandinistas started to
use the chant "Sandino yesterday, Sandino today, and
Sandino always,"[22] the hierarchy objected to this
symbolic use of Hebrews 13:8 and the substitution of
Sandino for Christ. Church supporters responded
"Christ yesterday, Christ today, and Christ always."
Thus a statement with which most Christians could
agree took on the ominous overtones of the divisions
within the Nicaraguan Christian community.

The Catholic hierarchy was also frightened by an
ideological statement which was formulated by a
Sandinista, Julio López, in October-November 1979.
López accepted the dogmatic Marxist view of organized
religion and argued that religion should be abolished
gradually in Nicaragua. To accomplish this, holidays
like Christmas should be taken away from the people.
While it was impossible to locate this letter, both
Sandinista supporters and critics concurred on the
contents of the letter.[23] Sandinistas argued that the
document never had the endorsement of or the approval

10

of the FSLN and was the product of an obscure and insignificant conference. More importantly, the statement was in direct contradiction to the <u>Official Communiqué Concerning Religion</u> which the FSLN present-ed in October 1980 and reaffirmed in August 1982.[24] However, given the perception of mistrust on both sides, it was not difficult to see how this statement would be interpreted as a signal that in time the Sandinistas would do away with the church as an institution.

Inasmuch as the hierarchy was afraid that Sandino would replace Christ and that the institution-al church would be gradually eliminated, they also feared that participation in the revolution and its process of reconstruction would replace participation in formal church activity. This fear had two con-cerns: the participation of Catholics in the mass organizations and the <u>CEBs</u> and the transfer of Nicaraguan Catholic customs to the revolutionary government.

For the traditional church, lay Catholic activi-ty is encouraged under the tutelage of priests who are loyal to the bishops. The <u>CEBs</u> were a problem for the institutional church, as was Catholic participation in the mass organizations, because it was difficult for the church to control the enthusiasm, commitment, and seeming autonomy of the Catholics in the <u>CEBs</u> and mass organizations. If these revolutionary Christians continued to unite grassroots Christian commitment to the poor with commitment to the revolution, the church was fearful that the government's authority would supersede that of the church.

All of these embryonic fears of the institution-al church seemed to come together in the celebration of the <u>Jornada Navideña</u> (Christmas Day celebration) in 1980. Traditionally, Christmas celebrations of the faithful were organized by the church or the individu-al family and epitomized the "popular religiosity" of Nicaraguan Catholicism. These customs, such as "<u>la Purísima</u>," which had developed over time in Nicaragua, were perceived to have been preempted by the govern-ment and the mass organizations in the celebration of Christmas.[25]

On November 26, 1980, Fr. Edgar Parrales, Minister of Social Welfare, announced the introduction of the <u>Jornada Navideña</u> to the Nicaraguan people. According to Fr. Parrales, the Social Welfare Ministry would take part in the celebration of Christmas and see to it that every Nicaraguan child received a toy or a game for Christmas.[26] Fr. Parrales spoke of the past when Christmas was viewed in a very material way and few children received many gifts while others received none. This Christmas, however, no child, rich or poor, would be deprived of the happiness of Christmas; each would receive at least one gift. To help in the distribution of gifts, the Ministry of Social Welfare would ask for the volunteer services of the mass organizations, the Sandinist Defense Committee (CDS). This new custom has been maintained since 1980.[27]

The response of the episcopate was to issue a call for a week-long festival of the Purísima[28] in Masaya. The celebrations would begin with the traditional "gritería" in honor of Mary, a procession, and would include such timeless Catholic practices as a recitation of the Holy Rosary at an outdoor mass. The week would end with a public celebration of first communion for the children of Masaya.[29]

La Prensa also printed the statement of the Center for Religious Studies which criticized the "Sandinist Christmas holiday" and accused the government of violating articles 5 and 9 of the Official Communiqué Concerning Religion. Article 5 of the Communiqué stated that religion cannot be used for political or commercial ends, while article 9 guaranteed the personal nature of religion. The Center asked why "the bishops who are our ties to Christ and the apostles were not consulted? Why wasn't any group or parish involved with the organization of our church consulted?"[30]

Finally, it must be emphasized that the doctrinal position of the Center for Religious Studies was traditional and emphasized the universal and institutional nature of Catholicism:

> Christ does not belong to any nation, he came from beyond the earth, the Nicaraguan Christ came from outside, brought by missionaries and is maintained by union with other churches of the world, especially the Catholic Church of Rome, whose leader, the Pope, is also our leader. This glance at the supernatural nature of Christ and his universal message should never be lost from sight . . . .. The Christmas celebration has been converted into a popular political theatre.[31]

Despite this background of potential mistrust between church and state, both actors approached each other cautiously but positively. The FSLN, in the aforementioned Official Communiqué of the National Directorate Concerning Religion, of October 1980, stated that Christian patriots had been and continued to be an integral part of the Sandinista Revolution. The efforts of individual Christians, the revolutionary commitment of Catholic priests such as Gaspar García Laviana, and the denunciation of the abuses of the Somoza regime by Catholic bishops such as Obando y Bravo, all contributed to the Sandinista victory.

The Communiqué emphasized the government's commitment to "religious faith as an inalienable right of the people which the Revolutionary government fully guarantees."[32] The FSLN also expressly rejected the traditional Marxist view of religion as the "opiate of the people":

> Some authors have stated that religion is a mechanism that alienates people and that serves to justify the exploitation of one class by another. This affirmation undoubtedly has historic value insofar as in distinct historical periods religion served as a theoretical support for political domination. Suffice it to mention the role that missionaries played in the process of domination and colonization of the indigenous of our country.
>
> Nevertheless, the Sandinistas affirm that our experience shows that when Christians, supported by their faith, are capable of responding to the needs of the community and of history, their same beliefs push them toward revolutionary militancy. Our experience shows us that one can be a believer and at the same time a conscientious revolutionary, and that there is no insurmountable contradiction between the two.[33]

The Church, for its part, issued a pastoral statement, "Christian Commitment for the New Nicaragua," on November 17, 1979, which firmly supported the revolutionary process and the development of direct popular democracy by means of a national dialogue, and endorsed the social analysis and theological positions taken at the 1968 CELAM conference at Medellín. This statement is the strongest the Nicaraguan bishops have made in favor of the poor and in defense of Nicaragua's right to seek its own solution to the problems of development.[34]

In anticipation of the fear many Nicaraguans might have had of the socialist aspects of the reconstruction process, the bishops distinguished between two types of socialism, one false and the other humanistic:

One hears that the Nicaraguan process is marching toward socialism. They ask the bishops what we think of this.

If, as some think, socialism discredits itself by taking from men and nations, their character as free protagonists in history; if it tries to submit the people blindly to the manipulations and dictates of those who arbitrarily hold power, such spurious or false socialism, we cannot accept. Neither would we be able to accept a socialism that tries to take from man, the right to the religious motivations of life or the right to publicly express these motivations and convictions publicly, no matter what the religious faith might be.

Equally unacceptable would be the denial of the parents' right to educate their children according to their convictions, equally unacceptable would be the denial of any right of human beings.

If on the other hand, socialism signifies as it ought to signify, the preeminence of the interests of the majority of Nicaraguans and signifies a unified and progressively participatory model of national economic planning, we have no objections. A social project that guarantees a common use for products, and resources of the country and permits, that upon that base, the satisfaction of the fundamental necessities of all, if socialism means a social project where the quality of human life improves, that seems to us just.

If socialism implies a growing diminution of injustice and traditional inequalities between city and countryside, between payment for intellectual and manual work, if it signifies participation of the worker in the products of his labor, overcoming economic alienation, there is nothing in Christianity that implies a contradiction with this process. Pope John Paul II indicated in the U.N. speech, the problems caused by the radical separation between work and property. If socialism supposes that power will be exercised from the perspective of the large majority and that power will be shared increasingly by an organized people, so that (society) will move toward a true transference of power toward the popular classes, again we will

14

find in our faith nothing but motivation and support.[35]

Post-Revolutionary Disagreements: 1980-1982

It is difficult to pinpoint with precision when the mutual distrust between the church hierarchy and the Sandinista government evolved into open hostility, but given the hierarchy's doctrinal preference for a harmonious, nonconflictual society in which reform should be gradual and guided, the break occurred when the hierarchy realized that the Sandinista government did not intend to institute exclusively liberal-democratic reforms.

The decisive period in this regard was April 1980, when both Alfonso Robelo and Violeta Chamorro resigned from the Junta of Government within days of each other. While Mrs. Chamorro resigned citing reasons of health, Robelo made no secret of his criticism of the Marxism and "totalitarianism" of the government and of the formation of the Council of State. Robelo and others in the private sector hoped that the Council of State would be a check against the FSLN.

However, Robelo was disturbed by the postponement of the formation of the Council of State from June 1979 to April 1980. When the Sandinista proposals were finally presented, they called for an enlargement of the Council from thirty-three to forty-seven members. They maintained that newly organized groups such as the Association of Rural Workers (ATC), which were not originally considered for representation, should be included. To Robelo, this was an attempt to give the Sandinistas a majority on the Council, and he resigned in protest from the Junta. Although Robelo was replaced on the Junta by another member of the private sector, Rafael Córdoba Rivas, the spring of 1980 was critical because it revealed clearly the nature of the opposition to the Sandinista government within the bourgeoisie. These events also revealed the identification of the Church hierarchy with the upper-class opposition. In May 1980, the Council of State was formally inaugurated, and the Catholic hierarchy issued its first call for the resignation of the priests who held cabinet positions in the Nicaraguan government.

The participation of priests in government. By 1980, the Church was inevitably caught, despite its universal doctrine, in the polarizations of Nicaraguan society between rich and poor, between Sandinistas and non-Sandinistas, between its own "base" and hierarchy.

15

While the base of the church wanted to participate in the revolution, the hierarchy believed that the Church should maintain a separate identity.

These divisions over authority and revolutionary participation were most evident in the problem of the priests in government. Although 200 priests, nuns, and religious figures held positions in government-related programs, controversy surrounded the high-level political work of several priests: Miguel D'Escoto, Minister of Foreign Relations; Ernesto Cardenal, Minister of Culture; Fernando Cardenal, Director of the Sandinista Youth; Edgar Parrales, Nicaraguan delegate to the OAS; and Alvaro Argüello, representative of the Nicaraguan Council of Clergy (ACLEN) to the Council of State until June 1983.[36]

Their visibility implied substantive as well as symbolic importance and crystallized the conflict of authority among five actors: 1) Archbishop Obando and the conservative faction within the Nicaraguan hierarchy; 2) the priests themselves, who were asked, in effect, to choose sides; 3) the Nicaraguan government, which requested the services of these priests and still needed their expertise; 4) the laity, who through the Christian base communities, had affirmed the Christian revolutionary work of these men; and 5) the Vatican, whose role had been important yet ambivalent.

The first call for the resignation of the four priest-ministers came in May 1980 when the Pastoral Communiqué of the Episcopal Conference argued that:

> The exceptional circumstances have passed, and Christian laity can occupy the political offices with no less efficiency than the priests who are presently occupying them.[37]

This call was to be repeated one year later (June 1, 1981) with increasing harshness of tone. At this time the Episcopal Conference demanded the resignation of the priests in a terse communiqué which revealed the espicopate's sense of threatened authority, and in the confrontational tone of the directive:[38]

> In reference to the participation of the priests in partisan politics and in public office we have said as Pastors of the Church and in its behalf, we feel "the duty to orient the priests, religious and all the People of God since the Bishop must be considered as the great priest of his flock, from whom derives and from whom

16

depends in a certain way the life of Christ in the faithful."

We declare that if the priests who are occupying public office and are exercising partisan responsibilities do not leave these positions as soon as possible, in order to incorporate themselves totally to their specific priestly ministry, we will consider them in open rebellion and formal disobedience to the legitimate church authority liable to the accepted sanctions within the laws of the church.[39]

Although this communiqué was signed in the name of the Episcopal Conference and implied unanimity among the bishops, one bishop, Rubén López of Estelí, stated later in an interview that he did not agree with the contents of the communiqué. Moreover, Bishop López said that he had not been informed of the nature of the message, even though he had participated in a bishops' meeting the day before the letter was released to the press.[40] Also, it appears that the Priests' Council, an advisory group to the Episcopal conference, was not consulted before the release of the letter.

For the conservatives in the Catholic hierarchy, the presence of the priests in government was a continual reminder that the Church had not maintained a separate identity from the revolution they distrusted. The priests' presence also gave a credence, nationally and internationally, to the government's position of religious tolerance. It was an affirmation at the highest levels of the participation of "pastors of the church" in the government. If these men were lay Catholics, their participation would be more palatable to the hierarchy and more consistent with the teaching of Puebla and of the 1971 Synod of Bishops. As priests they were entrusted with greater responsibility because of their divine calling and their ministry of the sacraments. As priests they were in the line of succession to become bishops and cardinals. Thus they potentially constituted the future magisterium of the church, which in the Catholic tradition must uphold the universal teachings of the church.

The doctrinal justification for the removal of the priests from office as well as the concept of the "exceptional circumstances" is to be found first in the 1971 statement of the Synod of Bishops:

Leadership or active militancy on behalf of any political party is to be excluded by every priest unless, in concrete and

17

exceptional circumstances this is truly
required by the good of the community and
receives the consent of the bishops after
consultation with the priests' council and
if circumstances call for it, with the
episcopal conference.[41]

In the Latin American context these ideas were
endorsed at Puebla, clearly giving the Nicaraguan
Episcopal Conference a doctrinal basis for its
position:

Party politics is properly the realm
of lay people (GS:43). Their lay status
entitles them to establish and organize
political parties, using an ideology and
strategy that is suited to achieving their
legitimate aims.
In the social teaching of the Church
lay people find the proper criteria deriv-
ing from the Christian view of the human
being. For its part the hierarchy will
demonstrate its solidarity by contributing
to their adequate formation and their
spiritual life, and also by nurturing their
creativity so that they can explore options
that are increasingly in line with the
common good and the needs of the weakest.
Pastors, on the other hand, must be
concerned with unity. So they will divest
themselves of every partisan political
ideology that might condition their judge-
ment and attitudes. They then will be able
to evangelize the political sphere as
Christ did, relying on the Gospel without
any infusion of partisanship or idealiza-
tion. Christ's Gospel would not have had
such an impact on history if he had not
proclaimed it as a religious message: "The
Gospels show clearly that for Jesus anything that would alter his mission as the
Servant of Yahweh was a temptation (Matt.
4:8; Luke 4:5). He does not accept the
position of those who mixed the things of
God with merely political attitudes (Matt.
22:21; Mark 12:17; John 18:36)" (OPA:1,4).
Priests, also ministers of unity, and
deacons must submit to the same sort of
personal renunciation. If they are active
in party politics, they will run the risk
of absolutizing and radicalizing such
activity; for their vocation is to be "men
dedicated to the Absolute."[42]

18

The response of the priests to these calls for their resignation was also disturbing to the conservative faction of the hierarchy. While the priests were respectful of the bishops, they were also firm in their refusal not to concede to these demands. Their very denial seemed to confirm the hierarchy's worst suspicions of their loss of authority in a changing church. The priests consistently responded that, in their judgment, the exceptional circumstances were not over and, moreover, they did not see any contradiction between "faithfulness to the church and faithfulness to the poor."[43] A year later, when asked a second time to resign, the priests responded, "We declare our unbreakable commitment to the Popular Sandinista Revolution, in loyalty to our people, which is the same as saying, in loyalty to the will of God."[44]

The response of the government to the May 1980 request was to send a delegation to the Vatican and to publicly laud the priests for the quality of their service. It is testimony to the importance given to this issue that a comprehensive response was included in the Official Communiqué Concerning Religion of the FSLN. First, the government guaranteed the right of all Nicaraguan citizens regardless of their civil status to participate in the political affairs of the nation. With regard to clerical participation in government, the government stated:

> The priests who hold office in the Government, heeding the call of the FSLN and their civic obligation, have done an extraordinary job so far. Confronted as it is by large and difficult problems, our country needs the cooperation of all its patriots, especially those who had the possibility to receive a higher education, which was denied to the majority of our people. That is why the FSLN will continue demanding the participation in revolutionary works of all those religious and lay citizens whose experience or qualifications are necessary for our process. If anyone of these religious persons decides to give up their governmental responsibilities due to personal reasons, that, too, is their right. To exercise the right of participation and to fulfill patriotic obligation is a matter of personal conscience.[45]

A year later when the bishops issued an ultimatum to the priests, the government's response again was to present their case to the Vatican. Sensing that the issue was at a standstill, both the

19

government and hierarchy sent delegations to Rome in an attempt to gain support for their respective positions.

Archbishop Obando y Bravo made several trips to the Vatican during the years 1980-1982. It is interesting to note that two of Obando's trips to Rome preceded the publication of the bishops' requests for the priests' resignations. In April 1980 he visited Rome, and the first request for resignation came in May 1980.[46] In May 1981, Obando visited Rome, where he spoke with the Vatican Secretary of State, Cardinal Casaroli, and with the Pope. In June 1981, the Episcopal Conference released its confrontational request for resignation. In the aftermath of this request and the priests' opposition, Obando returned to Rome to plead his case at the same time (June 8-12, 1981) that a high-level delegation from CELAM, headed by then Bishop López Trujillo, travelled to the Vatican to discuss Central America. López Trujillo reported that he was pleased with the results of these meetings where they talked with Cardinal Baggio of the Pontifical Commission for Latin America. The consensus of their meeting was that the Nicaraguan priests should resign from government.[47]

Meanwhile, the government too sent its high-level delegation -- consisting of Miguel Ernesto Vigil, Minister of Housing; Roberto Argüello, President of the Supreme Court; and Emilio Baltodano, of the FSLN -- to Rome on two occasions to discuss church-state relations. The government delegation was in Rome in August 1980 and in June 1981, immediately following the CELAM delegation. On both occasions, the delegation met with Cardinal Agostino Casaroli, Vatican Secretary of State, and on both occasions was told that the issue must be resolved within Nicaragua:

> Our concrete mission, affirmed the President of the Supreme Court of Justice, "was to expose to the Vatican the situation of Nicaragua and the opinion of the government regarding the same . . ... I understand that, with respect to the priests who are in the government, it is the bishops who have to resolve the situation, taking into consideration each particular case.[48]

Realizing that the Vatican would not resolve this dispute for them, the Episcopal Conference and the priests reached an accommodation on July 15, 1981. According to the statement of the bishops, the priests were to maintain their faith "in communion with the hierarchy," and a state of temporal exception would be conceded under the following conditions: "That while they exercise their public offices and performance as party functionaries they will abstain from all performance of all priestly duties, in public or in private within the nation or internationally."[49]

Predictably, the Christians who worked in the CEBs were extremely supportive of the priests' services. If one can measure public opinion by editorials and letters sent to Nicaragua's three daily newspapers over the course of two years, the majority of responses in El Nuevo Diario and Barricada were in favor of the continued service of the priests. The revolutionary Christians defended the priests because they remembered their active participation during the revolution. The revolutionary Christians also realized that the removal of these priests from office could severely weaken the commitment of the Nicaraguan church to the poor.

As a result of the temporary resolution of this crisis, the government, intent on keeping the channels of communication open and preventing further attenuated conflicts within the hierarchy, initiated a regular forum, The Permanent Commission for Dialogue, for discussion with the bishops. The government representatives were junta members Daniel Ortega, Sergio Ramírez, and Rafael Córdova Rivas, and René Núñez of the FSLN. They were joined by Bishops Julian Barni, López Ardón, and López Fitoria. Lamentably, this communication was terminated in February 1982 as a result of a bishops' letter which severely criticized the Nicaraguan government and its handling of the Misquito Indians.

The Misquito relocation. In January 1982 the Nicaraguan government undertook a massive relocation of 8,000 Misquito Indians from the area along the Honduran border to the interior of the country. While the Nicaraguan government justified this relocation because of the danger of raids from Honduras into the Misquito camps and the defense of the national territory, much international controversy focused on this relocation. Opponents of the Sandinista regime accused the Nicaraguan government of gross violations of human rights, executions of Misquitos, and forced relocations under adverse and restrictive conditions. In the midst of accusations and counteraccusations the Episcopal Conference of Nicaragua issued a statement which read in part:

> If it is possible to explain militarily the massive evacuation of these villages, we nevertheless must lament, from a human and Christian point of view, the displacement of the indigenous groups, who

21

have resided in these regions from time immemorial. Their displacement has been both to the settlements established by the government in the interior of the Republic and to Honduran territory where many have fled. Perhaps they were driven by fear or by what at times were drastic measures by which the former were moved to the mentioned settlements.

We recognize the right of the government authorities to use the measures necessary to guarantee the defense and integrity of the national territory. At the same time, we recognize the autonomy of the State and its right to determine the implementation of emergency military measures in all or part of the national territory in order to insure the defense of the country. Nevertheless we wish to remind everyone that there are inalienable rights that may not be violated under any circumstances and we state with sad surprise that in some concrete cases there have been serious violations of the human rights of individuals, families, and even entire villages.[50]

Within days, the Nicaraguan government responded with equal harshness in their rejection of the bishops' accusations. They accused the bishops of undermining the climate of national unity and of disregarding the mutually agreed upon Permanent Commission for Dialogue. The government also rejected allegations of serious violations of human rights,[51] and asked the bishops why they had not mentioned in their letter the documented participation of Catholic deacons and Moravian pastors in armed counterrevolutionary activity. Most important, the government stated that the bishops had been invited to visit the resettlement areas and had not responded to the invitation, thus implying strongly that their documentation was faulty.

In an analysis of this letter, what was striking was its lack of pastoral or spiritual quality. It was a political statement lacking Biblical references or references to Catholic social teaching.

While the letter was signed in the name of the Episcopal Conference, there is speculation as to whether all the bishops concurred. In particular, speculation surrounds the concurrence of Bishop Schlaefer of the diocese Bluefields, an area which includes part of the Misquito community. The week before the release of the bishops' letter, Bishop

Schlaefer was personally invited to accompany the Minister of Housing, Miguel Vijil, to the Misquito Coast and to the resettlement area of Tasba Pri, where the Housing Ministry had supervised plans for housing construction.[52] Bishop Schlaefer declined the invitation. However, in the course of their lengthy conversation, Bishop Schlaefer expressed his concerns for the Misquitos on the Honduran border, because the Río Coco was a problem. The river was too close to the lands they farmed, and frequent flooding occurred. According to Vigil, Schlaefer hesitated to act on a relocation because he knew that the Misquitos would resist removal from their ancestral homeland.[53] In the government's view, Bishop Schlaefer knew that the Misquitos had to be moved even before the border became a controversial war zone.

Because the government realized that Bishop Schlaefer was more informed than the other bishops about the living conditions among the Misquitos, they met with him several times after the publication of the bishops' letter to question him about the letter, the timing of its publication, and, most important, its evidence.

As for the question of allegations of serious violations of human rights in the letter, the bishops did not have firsthand evidence and did not adequately establish the sources of their secondary evidence when questioned. For example, the Protestant Development Committee (CEPAD), whose personnel, without the permission of its directors, had used CEPAD vehicles to transport supplies to counterrevolutionaries, had an interest in establishing the veracity of events on the Honduran border. Communications between CEPAD and the hierarchy did not reveal the source of episcopal evidence.[54] In my conversations with Archbishop Obando concerning this issue, the archbishop insisted that they had evidence and that it had been supplied by North American priests "who informed us through Schlaefer of maltreatment."[55]

Archbishop Obando also maintained that after the release of the letter the government "took Schlaefer from Bluefields, from his diocese on two occasions to question him. The Episcopal Conference had to intervene to obtain his release." When questioned, Obando denied that Schlaefer had been imprisoned by the government but he said that Schlaefer had been "sequestered by the government."[56] Bishop Schlaefer himself issued a statement saying that he had never been imprisoned in Nicaragua or anywhere.[57]

Undoubtedly, the release of the Misquito letter was a mistake on the part of the hierarchy and served to increase the tensions between the government and the hierarchy. Dialogue broke down, and the government again sent a special mission to the Vatican during April 1982. Continuity in the delegation was maintained by the selection of Roberto Argüello and Miguel Vigil, who were joined by Carlos Tünnerman, Minister of Education, who replaced Emilio Baltodano on this trip. Again the Nicaraguan delegation met with the Vatican Secretary of State, Cardinal Agostino Casaroli, and Mons. Silvestrini, Secretary of Foreign Relations.

The role of the Vatican Secretary of State was a positive factor in the amelioration of church-state tensions within Nicaragua. Cardinal Casaroli tried to mediate the personal and doctrinal differences between the Sandinista government and the conservatives in the hierarchy. At the same time, he lent his support to the Nicaraguan government. His role was instrumental in the continued service of the priests as ministers as well as in the appointment in June of two moderate Catholics as bishops. Mons. Carlos Santi was named bishop of Matagalpa, and Mons. Julian Barni was named bishop of León. Bishop Santi came from the parish of Darío, where Christian communities flourish. Bishop Barni, although at times critical of the government, was a constructive critic whose honesty was respected. Also, the Pope named[58] Mons. Pedro Vílchez as the prelate of Jinotega. Mons. Vílchez, who had previously worked with Bishop Barni, became bishop of the newly created diocese of Jinotega. These men showed themselves to be more amenable to dialogue with the government. Mons. Santi clearly distanced himself from conservatives in the hierarchy when he stated during his first homily as bishop, "Anyone who says there is no religious freedom in this nation is a liar."[59]

If the Misquito letter was a turning point in worsening church-state relations, further deterioration occurred during Holy Week in 1982, when Archbishop Obando y Bravo delivered a sermon which insulted the Sandinista government. The archbishop said that Jesus did not call Judas "brother" as he did the other disciples, but instead Jesus called him "compañero,"[60] which the archbishop said means "traitor." Compañero is a special word to the Sandinistas because it expresses not only friendship but also solidarity with the revolution. While "compañero" cannot be translated as "traitor" and never acquired the meaning of "traitor" in the Bible, the insult to the Sandinistas was clear and offensive.

Interior Minister Tómas Borge responded in kind to the archbishop's sermon a month later with a speech he delivered at the Second Congress of the World Christian Conference for Peace in Central America and the Carribean, May 26-31, 1982. In a speech entitled

"The Revolution Fights Against the Theology of Death,"
Borge personally criticized the Archbishop:

> In Nicaragua I believe that only now
> have Christians recovered the original
> meaning of charity, the true meaning of
> sharing (compañerismo). This reminds us of
> the distortion that a high official of the
> church made recently of the word companion.
> He said that Christ had called his disci-
> ples "brothers" and he only called as
> companion, Judas, the traitor. I believe
> that the person who said that is ignoring
> or pretending to ignore the true meaning of
> companion. Companion is one who shares,
> companion is one who offers, one who is
> capable of sharing his love, his charity,
> and even his life. With the word companion
> on their lips thousands and thousands of
> Christians died in Nicaragua, those who
> share the Holy Eucharist and who work
> together call themselves companions. A
> mother is a companion to her children,
> brothers are companions, even though at
> times there are brothers who are not
> companions, like Carlos Fonseca and Fausto
> Amador and Cain and Abel. Judas Iscariot
> would never have been a friend of Christ.
> I believe that he who said that is a
> militant counterrevolutionary, who aspires
> to be the Antichrist.[61]

In a concluding statement entitled "Who Persecutes and Kills Priests?" Borge was equally harsh in
his criticism of the intentional relocation of progressive priests and nuns in the archdiocese of
Managua. The Interior Minister also objected to the
archbishop's attempts to pressure the superiors of
foreign orders to transfer their priests or sisters if
they openly sympathized with the revolution:

> In other countries of Latin America
> priests identified with their people are
> assassinated, tortured, disappeared or
> expelled. Mons. Romero is not the only
> priest assassinated in Latin America even
> though his death was a magnificent illumi-
> nation of light and blood. In all of Latin
> America progressive priests are expelled,
> including Nicaragua. But, who in our
> country has expelled these priests and
> progressive nuns? It has not been the
> revolutionary government that has expelled

them, but it has been the theologians of
death. Who persecutes progressive priests
in Nicaragua? It has not been the
Sandinista Police, so slandered in the
elegant temples of the bourgeoisie, but it
has been the theologians of death, it has
been Torquemada. Some religious organizations seem to be the Holy Tribunals of the
Inquisition, in spite of the fact that in
these high organizations, we must be fair,
there are sensible, patriotic and Christian
elements.[62]

THE DIVISIONS AMONG THE BISHOPS

While the divisions between the hierarchy and
the government were clear, what was less evident was
that after the revolution the bishops themselves were
divided. Before the revolution, one could discover a
common tone, a uniformity of message in the bishops'
letters. In the two years immediately following the
triumph, despite a high degree of public unity,
doctrinal and political differences became apparent in
their letters. A comparison of two letters should
suffice.

The bishops' response to the FSLN Official
Communiqué Concerning Religion (October 7, 1980) was a
hostile and defensive letter which expressed fears of
"ideological control of the revolution" and of the
"dogmatic rigidity of other previously known models."
The government was accused of encouraging atheism and
of provoking divisions in the church by "wounding the
shepherd to disperse the sheep."[63]

In an oblique criticism of the power and legitimacy of the government, the bishops warned that power
might be used as a weapon against the people:

But not only in the area of church-
state relations, but in other aspects of
socio-economic and political life. Political Groups (i.e. the government) must
define, without reticence, their positions
and ideas. If they do not, the People will
not succeed in participating 'freely and
deliberately' in the process of their own
History. The People will always be at the
mercy of groups and systems of violence
vented upon defenseless majorities. The
rights of Power cannot be understood in
another way, except as they are based upon

26

respect for the objective and inviolable rights of man.[64]

The following week (October 22, 1980) the Episcopal Conference released another document, this one entitled "Jesus Christ and the Unity of His Church in Nicaragua." In contrast to the prior week's message, this letter was in part self-exploratory in tone and made an honest attempt to evaluate the unique role of Christ during this "historical moment" in Nicaragua. In an introspective tone, the bishops stated: "We are aware of the novelty of the historical experience that we are living; we find ourselves at the beginning of a new era in the life of Nicaragua. We believe that this moment gives us the possibility and responsibility to remake our nation from its foundation."[65]

What was most striking about this letter was its introspection and its accountability; the bishops had analyzed the problem of church unity in Nicaragua without strident criticism of the Nicaraguan government. In a section entitled " _Problemática_ of the Nicaraguan Catholic Church," the bishops acknowledged that:

> as a church _we_ [emphasis mine] have a serious problem, which is the doctrinal and moral confusion that exists in some church sectors . . . . Very special attention must be given to this problem.
>
> The Bishops of Nicaragua recognize that even though very positive steps have been taken in the pastoral field, _we_ [emphasis mine] must organize and improve even more our evangelizing work, in order to consolidate the unity of the Church and to breathe life into its apostolic action.[66]

It is difficult to assume common authorship of letters which are contradictory in perception of the revolutionary process, pastoral quality, and tone. In fact, it is difficult to assume even common agreement among the bishops, despite statements to the contrary.[67]

There was also evidence that the bishops as individuals had assumed different positions with regard to the revolution. Several of the bishops maintained cordial relations with the government. Bishop Schlaefer delivered the closing statement at the Council of State in 1981, and Mons. Barni delivered the opening address at the Council of State in 1982.

While the letters demanding the resignation of the priest-ministers were signed in the name of the Episcopal Conference, some bishops were more receptive to compromise. Mons. Barni, before he was named bishop, spoke with the priests and offered his services to obtain an extension from the Pope.[68] Bishop Schaefler also said that the Pope could grant exceptional circumstances in accordance with the Puebla documents.[69] As previously discussed, Bishop López Ardón was not informed of the 1981 letter.

The newest member of the Episcopal Conference, Mons. Vílchez, also expressed some support for the government. In an interview in Barricada, he voiced his agreement with the massive participation of Nicaraguans in the popular militias. According to the bishop, "if the United States invades Nicaragua, Nicaraguans have the right to defend themselves."[70] This is important because the popular militia was one of the mass organizations which was criticized by conservative members of the hierarchy.

Furthermore, in many of the dioceses the relations between the bishops, the Christian base communities, and the government officials were constructive. If one were to judge by the strength of the CEBs, one could infer that they had at least the tacit approval and in some cases the encouragement of their bishops. In the diocese of Estelí, the CEBs were thriving, and the government's relations with Bishop López Ardón were positive. In the diocese of Granada, under the direction of a more conservative bishop, López Fitoria, CEBs were not encouraged and church-state relations were strained, as they were in Managua.

While it was possible to discern these glimmerings of difference within the Episcopal Conference, it was also clear that the bishops themselves were concerned with their own visible display of unity and were unwilling to challenge openly the conservative members of the hierarchy, the most important of whom was Archbishop Obando y Bravo, former President of the Episcopal Conference. In the same interview in Barricada, Mons. Vílchez, while endorsing the popular militias, also said he would have no problem participating in talks with the government, "if [emphasis mine] the Episcopal Conference were to choose him."[71]

In Managua, church-state relations were most tense because of the fact that the capital city is the headquarters of both the government and the archdiocese of Managua. Miguel Obando y Bravo had been archbishop for thirteen years in Managua; he was a popular figure among both rich and poor, who remember him for his stand against the Somoza regime and who see him as the "head of the church" in Nicaragua. Obando was an outspoken critic of the government, especially since the state of emergency was declared on March 15, 1982. Because the news media were subject to prior restraint, the communications of the archdiocese, such as the Hoja Dominical, frequently disseminated news commentary which was critical of the government. For example, in June 1982, the Pope wrote a letter to Nicaragua's Catholic Bishops warning them of the danger to Catholic unity in the growth of the "popular church." The government initially, and mistakenly, stopped the publication of this letter in the national press. However, before the government reversed its decision, the letter had already been circulated by the archdiocese.

Relations were especially tense in Managua, where under the direction of priests and religious figures, the CEBs were strong and numerous. In July 1982, the strength of their convictions caused them to challenge the archbishop after his controversial transfer of a parish priest, Mons. Arias Caldera of Santa Rosa, a poor section of Managua. The people of Santa Rosa protested strenuously the removal of their pro-Sandinista priest and attempted several times to talk with the archbishop. After refusing repeatedly to meet with a delegation of parishioners, Obando finally consented to see them, but it was clear that no compromise was possible and that he would not reinstate the diocesan priest.

Tensions ran high because although this transfer was presented as "routine" by the Chancery office, in fact it was only the most recent of a series of transfers or removals of priests who sympathized with the government. One evening during a prayer vigil at the church in Santa Rosa, the auxiliary Bishop of Managua, Bosco Vivas, arrived and tried to remove the Blessed Sacrament. The people objected to these actions, and a skirmish occurred. The auxiliary bishop was a bit shaken up and the locked tabernacle fell to the floor. The next day the archbishop placed the church under an interdict and excommunicated those parishioners who had participated in the prayer vigil.

The Christians of Santa Rosa responded by challenging the excommunication, thus confirming, once again, the archbishop's fears that the base of the church was not sufficiently mindful of the bishop's authority. By the spring of 1982, the conservative faction of the Catholic hierarchy risked increasing isolation from the revolutionary process. Especially after the release of the Misquito letter of the Episcopal Conference and the transfer of Mons. Arias, the balance of forces had shifted to the government's advantage. However, two events intervened to stop the government's momentum in consolidating its Christian base of support and in improving relations with the moderate sector of the hierarchy: 1) the government's mishandling of the Bismarck Carballo affair, and 2) the papal visit of March 1983.

THE DELICACY OF CHURCH-STATE RELATIONS IN 1983

Bismarck Carballo, principal spokesman for the Archdiocese of Managua and director of Radio Católica, was involved in a scandal in early August. According to Fr. Carballo, he was having lunch with one of his parishioners when an armed man entered the house and forced him and his female parishioner to undress. The armed man then beat him, pushed him out the front door past a passing demonstration, and forced him into a police vehicle. He was held at police headquarters for several hours and was treated very poorly before being released.

According to the police version of this incident, the demonstration which was en route to the Argentine embassy was by chance passing the home of the lady parishioner when shots were heard. The crowd saw a man running out of the house, pursued by another man who was hitting him. The police took both men away in a police van, without realizing at the time that one of the men was Bismarck Carballo. Further investigation revealed a lengthy romantic relationship between the priest and his parishioner; what is unclear is whether the demonstration was spontaneous or planned.

In retaliation for Fr. Carballo's explanation, the Office of Communications Media of the Ministry of the Interior lifted its self-imposed ban on photos which were taken of Fr. Carballo running naked in the street. Archbishop Obando, a friend of Carballo, was compelled to defend him and accused the government of attacking the church through one of its priests. The publication of the pictures of Fr. Carballo was shocking to the majority of Nicaraguan people, who are quite conservative in their personal demeanor. In fact, the Nicaraguan people were more tolerant of the indiscretion of the priest than they were of the release of the pictures. While the government was certainly justified in responding to inaccuracies in Carballo's explanation, releasing these pictures was not the correct measure. The public's sympathy tended to support the priest and not the government.

This incident triggered a series of actions in support of Bismarck Carballo and counterprotests in Masaya and Managua. For example, a Salesian Catholic high school in Masaya was temporarily closed by the government after shots were fired in a skirmish, and the school's director was asked to leave the country.

After several days of discussion, the school was reopened, still under Salesian administration. The government did request that the school attempt to enroll both rich and poor Catholic students. After these events, the Episcopal Conference issued another letter, which criticized the government and warned that Catholics had the right to determine how their children were to be educated.

The Pope's visit to Nicaragua in March 1983 must be discussed within the context of the tensions between conservative and moderate forces within the Vatican. In retrospect, it is clear that by the time the Pope decided to include Nicaragua in his Central American itinerary, the conservative forces had decisively influenced him.

The Role of the Vatican

The Pope is informed by two conflicting sources of information concerning Latin America. On the one hand is the conservative leadership of CELAM and the Pontifical Commission for Latin America, under the direction of Cardinals López Trujillo and Baggio, respectively. On the other hand is the moderating influence of Vatican Secretary of State, Cardinal Casaroli. CELAM, after learning of the favorable report on religion and human rights in Nicaragua, released in October 1981 by Pax Christi International, compiled a very critical report on Nicaragua in January 1982. The CELAM report accused the Nicaragua government of Cubanization and of instrumentalizing religion, of trying to eliminate Catholicism, and of being overtaken by Marxism-Leninism. The appointment of López Trujillo as cardinal attested to his importance and credibility with the Pope.

Cardinal Casaroli, Vatican Secretary of State, met with the Nicaraguan delegations on three separate occasions, as well as with Bishops Obando and Barni. Casaroli had been a negotiator between church and state in Nicaragua and had successfully defused the issue of the priests in government on several occasions. At the same time, sensing the polarization that might lie in the future, Casaroli worked, in Vatican circles, to soften the CELAM interpretation of the Marxist threat to Catholicism in Latin America. The Secretary of State showed astuteness to the overriding issues of church-state relations which extended beyond the particularistic issue of priests as ministers in the Nicaraguan government. The larger issue was how the church should relate to political regimes which are not exclusively liberal democratic. Casaroli was aware of the fact that precedents might

31

be set in Nicaragua which might be used to improve the church's relations with regimes in Eastern Europe. Also, Casaroli showed more sensitivity to formulating the church's transnational role and was acutely aware of the fact that, historically, if church-state confrontation occurs, it is the church that suffers a loss of its (temporal) power.

Thus, there was a delicate balance of forces which seemed to shift from one side to the other within the Vatican.·· In December 1982, the Vatican announced that the Pope would not travel to Nicaragua unless the priest-ministers resigned. By late February 1983, this problem was again temporarily resolved, and the Pope's schedule included Nicaragua. In January 1983, López Trujillo was named Cardinal. Aggravating these two tendencies within the Vatican was the ambivalent role of Pope John Paul II.

Politically, the Pope was most distrustful of a Marxist state and its willingness to allow the institutional church to survive. When the Pope cautioned the Nicaraguan Catholic community against "unacceptable ideological commitments," the specter he saw before him was the dogmatic Marxism of his native Poland. Given his lack of familiarity with the Latin American reality, it was logical that he would be suspicious of any Marxist undertones that would threaten the institutional church. It was facile, though inaccurate, to see Nicaraguan Archbishop Obando y Bravo as a bulwark of Catholic unity against the Nicaraguan Marxist government in the same way that Cardinal Josef Glemp represented the Church against the Polish regime.

What was most threatening was the possibility of change within the institutional church. If the laity, in keeping with the directives of Vatican II, assumed more individual and collective responsibility, the relationships of authority within the church might change. The magisterium of the church might have to redefine itself -- its teaching role and its proper function. The church might become "democratized," and the unknown implications of such a change questioned the legitimacy of authority within the church. The Pope's strong denunciation of the "People's Church" during his visit must be understood within this context. In a previously mentioned letter to the Nicaraguan bishops, the Pope stated:

> In its most common acceptance, which appears in the writings of a certain current of theology, "People's Church" means a Church that arises much more from the free and gratuitous initiative of God. It means a church enjoying the autonomy of

32

the so-called bases, without reference to
the lawful pastors and teachers. Or it at
least means that such a Church set the
"rights" of the aforementioned "bases" over
the authority and charisma that faith lets
us see in the lawful pastors. Since the
term "people" easily takes on a markedly
sociological and political content, it
means a Church embodied in the popular
organizations, a church marked by ideologies placed at the service of 'popular'
claims and programs and groups which really
do not belong to the people. It is easy to
see and the Puebla document explicitly says
that the concept of "People's Church" can
but with difficulty avoid being infiltrated
by strongly ideological connotations, along
the lines of a certain political radicalization, of class struggle, of the accep-
tance of violence to achieve certain ends,
etc.

A "People's Church" opposed to the
Church presided over by the lawful pastors
is a grave deviation from the will and plan
of salvation of Jesus Christ. It is so
from the point of view of the Lord's and
the apostles' teaching in the New Testament
and in the ancient and recent teaching of
the Church's solemn magisterium. It is
also a principle, a beginning, of fracture
and rupture of that unity which he left as
the characteristic sign of the Church
itself, and which he willed to entrust
precisely to those whom "the Holy Spirit
established to rule the Church of God"
(Acts 20:20).[72]

Similarly, if the priest-ministers remained in
the government, this might help to establish a prece-
dent to be followed by other nations. To Pope John
Paul, the religious vocation was a calling which was
distinct and unique from all others, including the
political. The defiance of these five
priests-ministers threatened the accepted patterns of
authority in a church which, according to its doctrine, was above partisan politics. The Pope, in a
doctrinal sense, was a part of the scholastic tradition of Catholic thought. The church, in his view,
was obliged to strive to achieve the Thomistic vision
of the "common good" -- the good of all, which could
not be divided along partisan political lines.
Complicating any analysis of the Pope's position
is the distinction which must be made between his

doctrinal position and his humanity. The Pope believed strongly in the dignity of the human being.
One cannot misinterpret his forceful denunciation of
abuses of human rights and his strong pleas for social
justice in the Philippines and in Brazil. The Pope
had not hesitated to criticize the wealthy for their
complicity in the maintenance of widening disparities
between rich and poor. Yet he seemed resistant to
relate his advocacy of social justice to political
activity, especially when political action may involve
working with a Marxist government. During his recent
visit to Nicaragua, the "doctrinal side" of the Pope
was most in evidence, and he presented a doctrinally
conservative message to the Nicaraguan people. The
implications of this visit would be far-reaching and
were not in the best interests of the unity of the
Nicaraguan Christian community.

The Papal Visit in 1983

It must be said that neither the Pope nor the
Sandinista government conducted themselves with
diplomacy or skill on this historic occasion. It can
be argued on the government's behalf that they knew
beforehand what the Pope was going to say and were
therefore inclined to be less conciliatory. However,
Junta coordinator Daniel Ortega's welcoming speech at
Sandino airport seemed inappropriate and overly
political. The Sandinistas certainly had a legitimate
grievance against the United States, but the time to
present it was not upon the arrival of a Pope who was
uncomfortable with the political leanings of the
Sandinista government and whose visit had been in
doubt several times. A less belligerent welcome,
expressing respect for the Pope and thanking him for
his visit, would have been more appropriate and
reassuring. In fact, the Pope's misgivings seemed to
be confirmed at the outdoor mass he celebrated in the
July 19 Plaza. John Paul II was repeatedly inter-
rupted by Sandinista supporters who shouted "popular
power" when he strongly criticized the "popular
church." The government's lack of control of these
Nicaraguans made the Sandinista government vulnerable
to the charge of political opportunism.

Allegations were also made that more conservative Nicaraguan Catholics, under the direction of Fr.
Bismarck Carballo, tried to disrupt the crowd and
provoke a response from revolutionary Christians.
Some credence can be lent to this position because it
was alleged that the Pope was advised in a briefing
paper prepared for the Vatican that "the Sandinista
government is the enemy, any policy of accommodation

will fail.... A strategy based on strength, unity and firmness will therefore have greater chances of success than another giving first priority to good relations with the government."[73]

Unfortunately, the Pope's remarks did not contribute to refostering unity within the church or between the church and the government. By exhorting the faithful to obey their bishops, most noticeably Archbishop Obando y Bravo, the Pope displayed very little sensitivity to the divisions among the bishops themselves. Even if one were to follow the Pope's message and obey the bishops, the question could still be asked -- which bishops should be followed? Were the laity to follow those bishops who supported the revolution or those who become increasingly identified with the opposition?

In his attempt to bring unity to the church, the Pope aggravated the institutional crisis of Catholicism as well as the personal crisis of many Nicaraguan Catholics for whom his remarks were not sufficient. Those revolutionary Christians who participated in the CEBs and who were labelled by others as a "People's Church" or a "Parallel Church" could find no solace in the Pope's traditional message and his criticism of the "People's Church" as "absurd and dangerous." They did not consider themselves a parallel church; they resented this designation and maintained that they too were Catholics, and that they followed God's laws, practiced the gospel message, and received the sacraments of the church.[74] In a previous response to the Pope's aforementioned letter of June 26 to the Nicaraguan Bishops, some Nicaraguan Catholics argued:

> The truth is that we do not call ourselves "Popular Church." What has happened is that people have pinned us with this label in order afterwards to say that we are not Christians. But we ourselves have never used the term. When in your letter you described the way ecclesial communities should function, we felt that you were talking about those which already exist here. This is not to say that we are satisfied, that we do everything well, or that we are free from faults. Our ecclesial base communities are far from being truly committed, helpful, and united. But we know that a person is not converted to Christ all at once; instead, each day we must convert ourselves, or as our Bishops have said to us in one of their letters, "we make ourselves Christian by acting as Christians."[75]

In retrospect, it also seems clear that the Pope made some offensive and unnecessary remarks about recent events in Nicaragua. His extemporaneous statement that "I love the Misquitos because they are human beings" was followed by the slogan "Misquito power," which the Pope said in Misquito. Conceivably, the critical letter of the Nicaraguan bishops in February 1982 could have been excused since the reports of Americas Watch and the OAS had not yet been released. But both these later reports rejected the allegations of torture and genocide which had been made against the Nicaraguan government, and the Pope should have been aware of them. The Americas Watch report was issued in May 1982; the Pope lent credence to inaccurate claims in March 1983. It was difficult to see how these remarks would contribute to unity in Nicaragua. Moreover, as religious conflicts were increasingly political, controversial religious statements served to increase political polarizations.

It is a sad irony that a Pope who believed that the spiritual mission must remain separate from politics made an extremely political and divisive speech in Nicaragua. His attempt to unify the Nicaraguan church by an imposition of papal authority as a response to divisions within the church did not succeed. His visit split the Nicaraguan Catholic church more decisively than any other single action. As one priest said: "The Gospels are going in one direction, the Pope in another."[76]

The Consequences of the Papal Visit

In the latter months of 1983, the polarizations between the Catholic hierarchy and the base of the church became more profound, and dialogue between those who supported the revolution and those who did not was virtually nonexistent. Relations between the church hierarchy and the Sandinista government also deteriorated, although there was evidence that the government had learned how to respond in a more restrained manner to the accusations of the hierarchy. In general, what could be observed in Nicaragua was an increasing centralization of ecclesiastical authority in the Episcopal Conference and a concerted attempt by the Catholic hierarchy to weaken the bases of Catholic support for the revolution. Thus priests and laity who identified with the revolution were under great pressure to choose sides. Despite the compromise agreed upon in the summer of 1981, the four priests in government remained under strong pressure to submit governmental resignations or to risk losing their licenses as priests.

Those priests or religious figures who disagreed with the leadership role of Mons. Obando and the Episcopal Conference saw their authority greatly weakened. For example, after the papal visit, Father Francisco Oliva, S. J., participated in a television program in which he offered his opinion of the papal visit, stating that the Pope's presentation had saddened him and that he was frightened when he realized the degree of hatred which some Christians revealed toward the FSLN. In response to these statements, Mons. Obando withdrew the license of Fr. Oliva. It should be understood that while the validity of Fr. Oliva's priestly mission could not be taken away, the withdrawal of his license to minister the sacraments meant that he could not function as a priest. An example was set for other priests.[77]

The attempt to centralize authority within the Episcopal Conference also played a role in the dissolution of the Association of Nicaraguan Clergy (ACLEN) in the spring of 1983. This organization had been formed two decades earlier, during the period of Vatican II, in part to develop new liturgy, in part to explore, in an atmosphere of mutual support, the evolving role of the priesthood. As Somoza's human rights abuses increased, ACLEN gradually assumed a position critical of the government and supportive of the insurrection. When the FSLN triumphed, ACLEN was invited to join the Council of State. Despite opposition from the more traditional bishops, the Association voted to join the Council and elected a delegate, Fr. Felix Quintanilla, with Fr. Alvaro Argüello as an alternate. Almost immediately, the Episcopal Conference attempted to pressure ACLEN to withdraw from the Council in accordance with the wishes of the bishops.

Tension between ACLEN and the Episcopal Conference continued until May 1983, when the clergy received what was at first an unsigned communication from Rome asking them to change their statutes so that only priests born in Nicaragua could be members. According to the directive, the new statutes had to be approved by the General Assembly of ACLEN as well as by the Episcopal Conference which "was not obliged to give reasons for a possible rejection." Furthermore, the directive stipulated that the leaders of the Association should be selected first by their local bishops and "should not take part in any political, governmental or syndical institution." In conclusion, the directive also stated that "these obligatory modifications are not intended to give any official recognition to the Association, but are intended only to fix some limits upon action, limits which should be taken very seriously into account."[78]

Upon investigation, it was revealed that this directive came from Cardinal Oddi of the Sacred Congregation for the Clergy, upon the request of the Episcopal Conference. Rather than submit to these new rules, ACLEN was dissolved by a unanimous vote. If ACLEN's membership on the Council of State had been the issue of contention, dialogue and compromise should have prevailed.[79] Subsequently, CONFER, the Nicaraguan Association of Religions, received a similar request from Rome to revise its statutes.

Similar actions were taken against lay groups which were not political in their mission. Yet if their lay leaders identified with the revolution as well as with the church, they were asked to renounce their positions of leadership within the lay organizations. Many Nicaraguan Catholics, however, realized that the doctrinal position of the bishops was not in accord with the social teachings of the Catholic Church.

The overall result of the papal visit was to reinforce the authority of the Archbishop and the "spiritualist" views of the more traditional upper-class Catholics who opposed the revolution. At the same time, a sense of disillusionment was evident among Christians. Many sincerely wanted to work for reconciliation within their church but saw fewer and fewer opportunities for dialogue. They realized that without dialogue and reconciliation, an essential part of the mission of Christianity, the church would remain divided and younger generations of Catholics would be less willing to work within the institutional church.

Clearly, the polarization of relations within the Catholic church affected church-state relations. The Permanent Commission for Dialogue, established as a result of the controversy over the continued participation of the priests in the Nicaraguan government, was essentially moribund as of 1983. Yet it should have been clear by that summer that the major responsibility for the breakdown in relations rested with the bishops, strengthened by the Pope, who had moved to the offensive and did not see the necessity for dialogue.

The more liberal bishops were hesitant to challenge the archbishop and his supporters. To do so would have been a public acknowledgement that the unity of the bishops did not exist. Yet the divisions within the Episcopal Conference were clear and could be seen in the responses of the diocese of Estelí to the murder of Felipe and María Barreda.

The bishop of Estelí, Rubén López, was considered to be the most liberal of Nicaragua's bishops. Christian base communities thrived in this diocese, and many members of Estelí had travelled to other areas of Nicaragua to lend advice to new communities which wanted to establish Christian communities. Felipe and María Barreda lived in Estelí with their children and worked in the Christian community. They did political organizing and were members of the Pastoral Council of their diocese. As part of their commitment to the revolution, the Barredas volunteered to pick coffee two kilometers from the Honduran border. On December 28, 1982, they were captured along with four other workers from the Christian base community of Estelí, by a counterrevolutionary band. For six months the Nicaraguan government negotiated with the Honduran government to obtain the release of the Barredas, but to no avail. On July 16, 1983, the Nicaraguan government was informed that the Barredas had been killed.

Two weeks later, over 4,000 people attended a mass celebrated by more than thirty priests. Bishop López was not present at the mass because he had made previous plans. Yet it would be difficult to interpret his lack of attendance as a sign of the bishop's disapproval of the Barredas or what they represented to many Nicaraguans--an exemplary couple in the new Nicaragua. While the bishop did not attend the mass, he released a letter in which for the first time a member of the Catholic hierarchy publicly condemned the kidnappings and assassinations of many delegates of the word and members of the CEBs at the hands of the Somoza bands. The bishop's letter praised the Barredas because their lives had been exemplary of Christian love and they had offered their lives, as had many others, so that the new Nicaragua might be born. The letter also condemned the military and economic campaign undertaken against Nicaragua and expressed fears of an imminent war. Bishop López concluded by asking for the solidarity of other dioceses in the search for peace.[80]

In August 1983, relations between the Nicaraguan government and the Christian community reached a watershed when the social divisions created by the revolutionary process crystallized in the controversy over the law of Patriotic Military Service. In response to the increasing frequency and severity of the counterrevolutionary attacks, the government proposed a military draft law intended to increase the number of Nicaraguans who could be rapidly mobilized in an emergency situation. Beginning in October 1983, all males between the ages of 17 and 25 would have to register for the draft and would be required to serve two years of military duty.

Before this law had been discussed in the Council of State, the Episcopal Conference issued a

39

very strongly worded communiqué, "General Considerations on Military Service," in which they claimed that conscientious exemption from this law was a right that Nicaraguans could exercise because the law of Patriotic Military Service was designed to draft and indoctrinate young men into service not to the nation but to the Sandinista party, a party which they considered to be illegitimate, totalitarian, and distinct from Nicaragua's sovereignty.[81]

Other Christian groups came to the defense of the government, arguing strongly that the government was in fact legitimate and that obligatory military service was a legitimate power of the state and that if for religious or moral reasons a person was opposed to taking up arms he must accept some other form of service. In the bishops' letter, no other form of alternative service was suggested, leaving one with the impression that because the Nicaraguan state was, in their opinion, mistakenly confused with the Sandinista party, no obligation was necessary.

Furthermore, it was suggested in response to the bishops' letter that Vatican II did, in fact, establish a position of conscientious objection, which is a personal decision, even in the event of a nation's legitimate defense. However, conscientious objection did not question the legitimacy of the state.

Concerned Christians asked rhetorically why, if Nicaragua was such a totalitarian state, there were not repressive measures taken against the Episcopal hierarchy and why their letter was allowed the publicity it had received.

In terms of the unity of the bishops, there was evidence that not all the bishops were present when this communiqué was discussed and that not all agreed on the contents of this message. Bishop Santi argued that it was the duty of Christians to defend their nation and that he had not been informed of the communiqué.[82] Bishop Schlaefer also stated that Christians have the right to participate in their own national development.

The response of the Catholic hierarchy stood in marked contrast to that of many revolutionary Catholics and Protestants who recognized the need for the law. In the Protestant community one could also sense anxiety about the law and its implications, but the channels of communications were open between the government and Protestant leaders. To rally support for military service, the directors of the Protestant Development Committee, CEPAD, organized a well-attended meeting with René Núñez of the National Directorate of the FSLN. The meeting was open to the public and lasted for almost three hours; most of the time was devoted to questions which Cmte. Núñez patiently answered. It was clear that major queries centered on the haste with which the law had been drafted, the exclusion of women, and the overzealousness of the block leaders in "registering" people for the draft.[83]

The government's response to the criticism put forth by the Episcopal Conference was restrained. To counter the allegations of the law of military service's being "totalitarian," the government went to great lengths to explain the conscription procedures in other nations, such as Spain, Mexico, and Venezuela. In so doing, the similarities between the laws were made evident, and the case for opposition to the law was weakened.

There was some evidence that the government attempted to avoid unnecessary confrontations with the Catholic hierarchy. In April 1982, the government responded to the denials of Fr. Bismarck Carballo by releasing incriminating photographs of him to the national press. Yet, in August 1983, a weekly magazine of satire, Semana Cómica, was closed for one month by the government for publishing fiction concerning Bismarck Carballo. Improving relations between Fr. Carballo and the government would not account for the censure of Semana Cómica, but rather it was due to the government's realization that they did not want to further provoke the Catholic hierarchy and they did not want to increase the personal and political difficulties of revolutionary Catholics. Similarly, El Nuevo Diario was not allowed to publish a Mexican article concerning revolutionary Christianity in the CEBs.

Despite these tentative efforts on the part of the Sandinistas, tensions ran high among the people themselves. Skirmishes were reported between groups of revolutionary Christians and supporters of the archbishop. On October 9, 1983, the traditional procession in honor of the Virgin of Fátima erupted into fistfights between members of the Christian base community of a residential section of Managua, "Centroamérica," and supporters of Archbishop Obando. Anthony Quainton, the former American Ambassador, was marching in the procession with Mons. Obando. Members of their group carried placards saying "They shall not kill" and "I am a conscientious objector."[84]

Priests who refused to offer prayers for Nicaraguan patriots who had died fighting the counterrevolutionary bands were forced out of the barrios in which they ministered. Whether these protests were organized by the government through the Sandinist Defense Committees, as critics have alleged, was difficult to determine.[85] But it was also clear that the people themselves were capable of voicing their own protests without government encouragement, and at times the Sandinista government was compelled to restrain them.

CONCLUSIONS

The changes which began at Vatican II, which gave the laity a greater voice and made the church inclusive rather than exclusive, were in the process of fruition in Nicaragua. It was difficult for many in the church, especially in the hierarchy, to deal with the implications of Vatican II and Medellín. A changed and still changing church was profoundly threatening. Some Catholics appeared to find comfort in the retrenchment of Puebla, but many did not.

For Nicaragua's revolutionary Christians, it would be difficult to adjust to the devastation of the Pope's visit and his insensitivity to their revolutionary struggle. His unwillingness to pray for the souls of more than 700 Nicaraguans, many of them delegates of the word, who gave their lives defending the revolution from Honduran-based "contra" attacks, was deeply disturbing to many Nicaraguans.

Hope lay in the realization that the Nicaraguan revolution was made with Christian participation and that the revolutionary process was irreversible. Mistakes had been made by the government and the church in their attempt to work out a new relationship, but the process would continue. It would be fitting to close with the words of Bishop Vílchez, of the new diocese of Jinotega: "If the church and the government are working for the same end -- the well-being of the Nicaraguan people -- then we must be in dialogue together.... We want a Nicaraguan Christian Revolution; a socialist revolution open to God. Here there is religious liberty."[86]

RELIGIOUS INSTITUTIONS AND BOURGEOIS IDEOLOGY
IN THE NICARAGUAN REVOLUTION*

Luis H. Serra**

INTRODUCTION

Our objective here is to make a contribution to
the scientific understanding of the religious conflicts in the current Nicaraguan revolutionary process, and consequently, to contribute to the
elaboration of suitable responses to the imperialist
offensive in this ideological area. Our basic hypothesis is that the religious institutions have been
converted, at the present time, into the main mechanism to perpetuate the bourgeois ideology which
previously dominated and, in fact, held together the
Somocista society.

In order to be able to demonstrate this hypothesis, we start from an analysis of the ideological
apparatus during the Somoza era, when it clearly
appeared that the religious institutions were one of
the various transmitting mechanisms of the ideology
that established and perpetuated Somocista society.

The next step is to refer briefly to the changes
which occurred since the revolution and its possession
of political and military power in different ideological spheres. Here we see a contradictory process: on
the one hand, a large part of the religious institutions have been intensifying their identification with

* This chapter flows out of a paper presented at the
Third Nicaraguan Congress of Social Scientists,
Managua, October 1982. This study would have been
impossible without the cooperation of various individ-
uals involved in the Nicaraguan revolutionary process,
both Christians and nonbelievers. In particular, we
would like to thank Jorge Espinoza, Rafael Lucio Gil,
Ligia Pérez, Bertha Loyasiga, Zeneyda Bravo, Rosa A.
Hernández, Manuel Pinzón, Félix Navarrette, Daniel
López, Manuel García and the pleasant Sigrid.
** Translation by Laura Nuzzi O'Shaughnessy with the
diligent and generous assistance of Theodore F. Nuzzi.

the bourgeoisie (middle classes) and with imperialism, while on the other hand, the remaining ideological institutions have been developing a process of democratization and of the discovery of new values.

The third step consists of an attempt to explain scientifically how religious institutions serve the ideological expression of the middle classes who are allied with imperialism. On this point we indicate that the policies that one can devise to combat the imperialist manipulation of religion depend on the kind of explanation we can offer. The present period is rich, as much in wisdom as in shortcomings, in the treatment of this phenomenon.

THEORETICAL FRAMEWORK

We understand <u>ideology</u> as a system of ideas, values, beliefs and symbols expressing themselves in conduct and attitudes, which a social class elaborates specifically in socioeconomic formations in accordance with their interests.[1]

Ideology is part of the overall superstructure dialectically related to the infrastructure or means of production under the "determination in the final analysis" of the latter, but with characteristics and specific laws that some determine as having "relative autonomy" from the ideological field.[2]

The dominant classes elaborate an ideology that tries to conserve, to legitimate, and to reproduce the social relationships of production that benefit those classes, through falsification and clouding of objective reality. This ideology is dominant in a society in the measure by which the exploiting class controls the reproductive devices of false consciousness, which it subtly imposes in order to generate the consent of the dominated, avoiding in this way the need for coercion in order to maintain their power.[3]

These transmitting mechanisms or reproductive devices are principally the family, the school, the means of communication, religion, the diverse churches, and the political, labor, and social organizations. The key persons within these institutions have been given the name <u>organic intellectuals</u> by Antonio Gramsci.

Ideology is learned from early infancy in the social relationships of the home, which reproduce the relationships of dominant production, and in language which is saturated by a specific meaning. Those beliefs, ideas, and values are housed in the sub- and un-conscious levels of the psyche, thus attaining a hidden character, even for the individual who practices and sustains this ideology, or who does not

44

verbally propagate this ideology but practices it just the same.[4]

Within the ideological field, religion* has occupied a predominant place in precapitalistic societies. Historically, its predominance has decreased proportionately with the advance of capitalism, although this decrease has been greater in developed or imperialistic capitalist countries than in dependent or underdeveloped capitalist countries such as Nicaragua.[5] This is due to the fact that capitalism has developed other areas of ideology for its legitimation, such as classical political economy, liberalism, idealist philosophy, and positivism. Also, the reproduction of capitalist relationships of production are accomplished with less dependence on "extra-economic mechanisms" than were the means of precapitalist production.

Now, as we already pointed out, ideologies in any society have a direct relationship with the existing social classes and their struggles. Ideology, in its religious, artistic, and ethical aspects, cuts across the class struggle, and has internal contradictions. "The Church is in a world split into antagonistic social classes, as much on a universal scale as on the local level. . . . Christians belong to opposite social classes which means that social divisions cut across the Christian community itself."[6]

In this way, in the area of religion, we have, on one side, the dominant class trying to insure the fact that religion sanctifies and legitimates the status quo, using for its maintenance various mechanisms such as the suppression of institutions or religious competitors; privileges granted to supportive clergy; control over the training of the clergy; the adaptation of religious doctrines and practices; familial relationships with the hierarchies; economic, legal, or educational benefits; and political agreements. In short, the objective which has been historically attained by the dominant classes in class societies has been that of transforming religion into

---

*Religion: Sociologically, we understand religion as a "structure of discourse and practices common to a social group and referred to some forces (personified or not, multiple or singular) which the believers consider as foregoing and superior to their natural and social being, before which believers express feeling a certain dependence (expressed, governed, protected, etc.) and consider themselves obliged to maintain a certain behavior with their kind" (Otto Maduro).

"the opium of the people," a sleeping potion, for its conscience and a source of escapist illusion.[7]

On the other hand, the exploited class tries to express in the area of religion its interests, its living conditions, and its yearning for liberation. This expression depends on the correlation of forces and the degree of class consciousness and of popular organization.

The class contradictions that characterize religion become more acute in revolutionary times, as in the present Nicaraguan process. The objective of the exploited classes, rarely attained in history, has been to express through religion their "protest against real poverty," and even their faith has served as motivation in the revolutionary struggle. As the stage prior to the Sandinista triumph shows, "our experience tells us that when Christians relying on their faith are capable of responding to the needs of the people and their history, Christian beliefs themselves push individuals to revolutionary militancy."[8]

THE DOMINANT IDEOLOGY AND ITS REPRODUCTIVE INSTITUTIONS IN THE SOMOZA PERIOD

The dominant ideology of the Somoza period expressed the dependent capitalist, neocolonial character of Nicaragua's socioeconomic formation. Although ample sectors were tied to precapitalistic production relationships (subsistence, small business, tenant farming, day labor), these were clearly subordinate to capitalist accumulation. This ideology also represented the dictatorial character of the political system, and carried with it the heritage of three centuries of colonial Hispanic domination.

We now refer briefly to the characteristics of the principal ideological tools of Somocista society:

The Family

For the majority of the people who were underemployed and poorly paid, the family as a social unit was weak. Frequently, family members, including children, fended for themselves, often seeking employment far from home. This involved prolonged journeys and bad working conditions, and was affected by the cyclical rhythm that the agro-exporting economy imposed. This family instability was related to the specific means of production of the country (and drew its ideological strength from paternalistically predominant machismo) and to a patriarchal social

46

model. Family instability was exacerbated by the crude physical violence which reflected in the home the repressive conditions of the brutal dictatorship.[9]

Children, with a mortality rate of 120 per 1000 in the first year (due to the ominous mixture of illness, malnutrition, and lack of care), became abandoned beings. Mistreated, "educated in the school of hard knocks," they matured rapidly in the tough trades of vendors, shoeshine boys, and beggars, and frequently fell into vices and delinquency.

Extensive prostitution was a product of economic necessity, and of the weakness of the family, general corruption, and sexual repression, which in turn corresponded to repression in politics, labor, and education. Sexuality for women was simply an aspect of their reproductive functions, while for men it was a free activity that fell into licentiousness and sadomasochistic sexual relationships. This double standard was sanctioned by a civil code that permitted divorce for the most minor matrimonial infidelity on the woman's part, while requiring the wife of an unfaithful husband to provide proof that her husband was having an affair. Also, Somocista laws benefited lovers while discriminating against wives in matters of inheritance.

In addition to the general pressures that everyone felt, women saw themselves "obliged to experience even more dependence and submission before men. . . . Our role as women has traditionally been reduced to household work, an exhausting and enslaving job, a daily job that we women do without pay and that no one recognizes as important."[10]

To this, it is necessary to add the high percentage of women in domestic jobs who put in exhausting workdays for miserable salaries and had to put up with the power and abuses of the employer and his children, even to the humiliating extent of washing his dirty trousers. "To be poor and a woman meant you would have a 30% possibility of attending school. . . . Also it meant finishing childhood abruptly after a brief puberty with a first pregnancy, usually outside of marriage. . . . To be a woman of 34 years old meant to have been pregnant some 8 times, and that only 3 or 4 of these children would be alive."[11]

In this manner, the family, the first socializing institution of the dominant ideology for the new human being, served in the Somoza period to infuse aggressiveness, individualism, competition, and corruption. In conclusion:

"The dictatorship is socio-cultural because it has generated a group of social values

47

that affect the human roots of Nicaraguans. Corruption, opportunism, a cynical mentality, the appropriation and abuse of the State's resources, theft, assassination -- all of these anti-social values were developed in the 45 years of oppression."[12]

The School System

Various studies show that education during the Somoza period served two basic objectives: to legitimate the political-economic system and to train people to do the work it demanded. This system was characterized by limited access and poor educational quality. Its governing body, The Ministry of Public Education, has been defined as an arm of the Somocista party.[13]

The economic system (the agro-exporting character of Nicaragua's dependent economy) meant in the field of education that the majority would not be educated. Thus, on the one hand, Nicaragua had an elevated illiteracy rate (52%) and poor quality of scholarship, especially in the rural population. On the other hand, in order to satisfy the needs of the commercial, financial, administrative, and state sectors which were tied to the agro-exporting apparatus and to the weak industrial sector which developed in the 1960's because of the influence of the Central American Common Market and the cotton boom, technical and professional education was pushed under the guise of "modernization."

Thus the rural school prepared the agricultural workers and foremen; the urban primary school produced semi-specialized workers, or employees with little skill; the secondary school trained employees of a superior level, sometimes in technical skills; and the University forged professionals and technical administrators needed to manage the imported technologies or the state sector, or to supervise a business.[14]

On the highest level, the Central American Institute of Business Administration (INCAE) existed as a product of North American "cooperation" through the Alliance for Progress, where programs, professors, methods, and techniques depended directly on the U.S. The INCAE came to assume the function of a "Think Tank" for the dictatorship after the 1972 earthquake. Also, the Central American University (UCA) was created with the objective of "deadening revolutionary ideas and to ward off the influence of the radical student movements and to satisfy the human resource demands of local capitalism." Both institutions were controlled by the three major economic groups --

48

Banic, Banamer, and Somoza -- which depended in turn on important North American financial groups such as Rockefeller and Morgan.[15]

The Somocista state tried to develop education within the limits of the demand of the economic system, in order to avoid discontent and the radicalization of the exploited sectors who possessed some education and awareness of the economic system. But the inefficiency and poor quality of the school system and the consciousness-raising work of political groups such as the FSLN prevented the total domestication of students, who on several occasions opposed the dictatorship and the school system which represented it. Also, the teaching profession had memorable periods such as 1969-1972 when it endured the Somocista repression for defending its rights. Nevertheless, administrative control and ideological persuasion tended to form a corps of teachers which defended the dictatorship or maintained a passive conformity under the alleged "apolitical position" that Somoza claimed for the teaching profession.[16]

The intellectuals educated in this system spent their time participating in the theoretical and artistic discussions of the imperial metropolis. They attempted to distinguish themselves from the common people through the formalities of a sophisticated language, stylish clothing, and a rhetoric as encyclopedic as it was empty.[17] The university graduates hoped to obtain scholarships in the United States and to study in their great centers, contributing in this way to the "brain drain" that imperialism prompts as a traditional form of extracting resources from its neo-colonies.[18]

The dominant artistic trends imitated things "foreign." Here we speak of the trend that painted "the rural world as a strange and romantic territory" and the peasant as "ignorant, ingenious and uneducated." We refer to "modernism" that, in spite of its originality, "amply fosters the belief in the dominant European cultural ideal that the capitalist world showers upon Latin America," or we speak of the vanguard movement that in spite of its nationalist postures was supported by the dictatorship, according to some of its members.[19] Yet it should be known that the dictatorship was not really characterized by its devotion to artistic creation, as shown, among other things, by the meager budget of the Department of Cultural Extension of the Ministry of Public Education (MEP)[20] and the poor development of the School of Fine Arts.

That is to say, the institutions of education took charge of inculcating the values, concepts, and ideas which belonged to a dependent capitalism under a

49

dictatorial regime: academic competition, the private and individual appropriation of knowledge, obedience and submission to school authority, uncritical memorization of dictation, motivation of learning through fear or punishment, reverential respect for the teacher or for the most "intelligent," ambition to stand out individually, contradiction between the words "freedom" and "democracy" and the reality of the exploitation and misery of the country, the frustration and humiliation of the "less intelligent," and the drive to "pass" at whatever cost. Most seriously, the student learned of rigorous regulation, the imposition of norms, and the inability to change or participate in those decisions that affected him. All of this lead to depersonalization; that is to say, to act as others wanted without believing in or desiring it. Educational alienation was part of the general alienation of a people who tended to look at themselves and at reality through the eyes with which the bourgeoisie and imperialism looked at them.[21]

This ideological formation took place through authoritarian, paternalistic student-teacher relations, draconian regulations, and selective competitive evaluations. In spite of this, the school system was presented as a panacea for misery, as the channel for social mobility. In this way, based on partially verified evidence (a qualified worker could earn more than a nonspecialized worker), the illusion of social change by means of upward individual mobility was created. The ideologized school served both as an escape valve for social pressure and as a means of filtering and selecting the most skillful and humble of the people to collaborate with the dominant class and the system.

The Mass Media (MCM)

The Means of Mass Communication (MCM) have been considered as the most important device of "ideological transmission" of modern capitalism, given that in capitalist societies (U.S., Europe, Japan) practically the total population experiences mass communications, even in the intimacies of their rooms and psyches.[22] In Somocista Nicaragua, with one of the lowest per capita percentages of radios, TV, and press on the continent, and with a very high index of illiteracy, the MCM have not had the same priority as they do in the U.S., Mexico, or Argentina. Nevertheless, with "modernization" in the 1960's, under the impulse of the Central American Market, the Alliance for Progress, and the Yankee MCM programs for Latin America (to scare away the ghost of the Cuban Revolution), "practically no social sector could now be ignorant of the crushing weight of the propaganda machinery, which through transistor radios preach alike the virtues of free elections, Christian submission and the magic of analgesics. . . ."[23]

The most effective form of control of the MCM on the part of the middle classes was through ownership. Thus the Banic group, for example, controlled Telivicenter (TV 2 and 12) and Publicity and Promotions Inc., and was part of the governing board of La Prensa, UCA, and INCAE. For its part, the Somoza Group was owner of TV 6 and 8, the newspaper Novedades, and Radio Station X, and co-owner of Union Radio and Radio Managua. All the TV channels were affiliated with the American Broadcasting Corporation (ABC).[24]

Besides direct control, the middle class, by means of their financial control over advertising, succeeded in deciding the type of programming that was transmitted. Advertising prompted the consumer to buy superfluous items including harmful products such as alcohol and tobacco, manipulated the female body as a sex object in the sale of merchandise, and pushed the consumption of imported (North American) goods.

As for television programming, a study shows that the majority of programs were of North American origin; for example, on Channel 6, 85.41% of the programs were foreign, as were 76% on Channel 2.[25] Most of the programs were soap operas, serials, full-length features, and educational programs in which the "American way of life" was exalted. Television portrayed the "barbaric" redskins of North America being eliminated by the "civilized" white colonists, the threat of Soviet-Cuban totalitarianism and the dangers of atheistic communism, and the happiness that could be achieved with a Cadillac, a luxurious house, or a trip to Miami. The advertisements used sophisticated subliminal theories developed by "experts in motivational analysis" in order to manipulate human conduct to promote consumption and to think and, therefore, act in accordance with the interests of the transnationals.[26]

Along with the influence of TV and radio, an avalanche of magazines was produced for the adult public, such as Reader's Digest, Better Homes and Gardens, Cosmopolitan, Vanity, Vision, Good Housekeeping, Woman's Day, and Fascination. Others such as Superman, Batman, and Donald Duck (whose ideological message has been presented through his angelic appearance, according to the study done by A. Mettelard and L. Silva)[27] were designed for younger audiences. School texts were the famous USAID-ROCOL books, prepared by Yankee advisors as part of the Alliance against Progress, as Victor Alba christened it. These books were denounced during the 1960's as clearly contrary to the idea of nationality.[28]

The local bourgeoisie admired and imitated their foreign cultural patrons. They identifed with their imperialist masters as a means of differentiating themselves from the "plebs" and the "Indians." The fundamental characteristic of these dominant groups was their aspiration to be part of the dazzling metropolitan bourgeoisie, an aspiration that was a source of permanent frustration for them.[29] Historically, the dominant group first imitated the Spanish. After independence, the paradigm was French and English culture. In the present century, they imitated things North American and showed contempt for what was national. The imperialist represented "civilization" before the "barbarity" of the "uncultured Nicaraguan backwardness." The proposed remedy for backwardness, according to these bourgeois Nicaraguans, who would sell out their own country, was simply to import North American capital, to mix with "superior" races, to study their countries, to practice their customs -- in conclusion, TO BE LIKE THEM.

This ideological attitude conditioned, among other things, artistic expression, since the bourgeoisie became "the Maecenas of those artists who bring the latest styles. . . . The artist sees himself also pressured to renounce his identity as a Nicaraguan in order to be able to subsist."[30]

While the elite consumed the most exotic and new of the foreign "isms," the people developed a culture that, in its best expression, was protest. For most, popular culture was a mixture of the Hispanic inheritance with indigenous characteristics, and the ranchero culture of Mexican melodrama with its burden of violence, machismo, and daily resignation. In other words, it was "a dispersed, mutilated culture. . .with a great part of its possibilities destroyed in its development or in its embryonic stage."[31] This popular culture culminated in periods of insurgent popular movements such as the glorious rising of General Augusto C. Sandino, and more recently (since 1956) the "beginning of the end of the dictatorship" and the ascent of the masses.

The Somocista tyranny exercised a severe control on the MCM, except during exceptional periods when popular protests forced space for minimal "democratic" freedoms. Besides direct ownership, the dictatorship controlled the media through legislation (the famous "Black Code"), through the use of repression against revolutionary or simply honest intellectuals, and in more subtle ways through the monopoly on newsprint, the restriction of publicity, discriminating taxes on parts and machinery, or the denial of access to information[32] to journalists who were critical of Somoza.[32] In this manner, under the weight of a combination of controls, virtually all of the opposition press collapsed, with one exception: La Prensa,[33] which was the voice of the Conservative Party and of sectors of the bourgeoisie opposed to the dictatorship. La Prensa practiced honest and courageous journalism under the direction of Pedro J. Chamorro, until his assassination in 1978 and subsequent destruction of the newspaper's headquarters in 1979.

On the other hand, Yankee imperalism through the Agency for International Development (AID) and the United States Information Agency conducted research on the media, even including investigations that in a sophisticated manner studied the habits and ways of thinking of the Nicaraguan people in order to devise educational plans that benefited North American interests in the region.[34] In sum, the MCM of the Somocista period exalted consumerism, individualism, and anticommunism, and cooperated in the alienation of the people by inundating popular beliefs, values, language, and achievements with supermarkets, coffee shops, discotheques, Chiclets, and snobbism. It was Coca Cola and alienation!

The Religious Institutions[*]

The Catholic Church penetrated our country as part of the colonial Spanish state, on which it

---

[*] CHURCH: We understand the sociological concept of church as a group of actors and institutions that possess the legitimate exercise of religious power, and whose features are a) a large stable intergenerational and multiclass public, b) a body of beliefs and codified norms, c) a body of hierarchical leaders that determine doctrinal orthodoxy, and d) a position of importance in society (Otto Maduro). This sociological definition of "church" is more restricted than the theological definition that is taught to all those baptized as Catholics, whether they are laymen or religious (Vatican II, IG 31). SECT: We define a sect as a religious group chacterized by an amorphous structure of small membership, with strict rules of membership which are radically critical of other institutions, whose messages can be of the mystical or utopian type, and which does not affiliate with other religious groups (Christopher Hill, Sociology of Religions, Chapters 3 and 4).

depended for its appointments, its regulations, and
the collection of tithes, thanks to the relationship
of "patronage" between the Vatican and the Spanish
Crown. Except for a small minority represented by
bishops of the stature of Fray Bartolomé de las Casas
and Fray Antonio Valdivieso, the majority of the
colonial Catholic clergy were, consciously or uncon-
sciously, apologists for the dominant classes.[35] The
priests of the pre-Colombian period were a part of the
dominant classes, and religion fulfilled a key role in
the perpetuation of the social relationships of
exploitation.[36]

After independence, the Catholic Church was the
bastion of the Conservative Party then opposed to the
advance of liberal capitalism. In this way the church
was weakened during liberal governments and was
strengthened during Conservative periods when the
oligarchy of Granada ruled. Under Conservative rule,
in the "Thirty Years Period" from 1858 to 92, Catholicism was recognized as the "Religion of the State" and
enjoyed the same ideological monopoly that it had
during the colonial era. Through the Concordat signed
with the Vatican in 1867, Spanish _Patronato_ was
virtually reestablished. While the political, economic, and ideological power of the Church was severely
questioned by the liberal regime of Zelaya (1892-
1909), that institution recovered its power, with the
exception of its extensive landholdings, after the
Conservatives again took power in alliance with the
North American domination of Nicaragua (1909- 1926).[37]
It was during this era that Archbishop Monsignor A.
Lezcano, a member of the oligarchical Congress, from
the pulpit urged the people to participate in the
elections organized by the conservatives, and to
respect the government's authority "because all
authority comes from God." During this period in
which the glorious anti-imperialist struggle of
General Augusto C. Sandino was in progress the Episcopal Conference of Catholic Bishops tried to dissuade
the people from participating in those "deeds of
violence that lead to nothing" and to persuade them to
dedicate themselves peacefully to production.

After Sandino's death, the authorities of the
Catholic Church served as legitimators of the
Somocista dictatorship through indirect means, with
their silence and indifference, or by direct means,
through their cooperation in public acts, in liturgical celebrations which honored the dictator or members
of his family, such as the lamentable coronation of
his daughter with the symbols of the Virgin. A
declaration typical of the hierarchy's position, made
by the Episcopal Conference in 1950, should suffice:
"For Catholics, it should be a sure and exalted

doctrine that all authority comes from God, and that when you obey the government, you do not degrade yourselves, rather you perform acts which constitute obedience to God."[38]

Activities promoted by the Catholic Church through lay groups in the field of education, and through charity in hospices and asylums, objectively constituted--beyond the good intentions of the participants--a palliative; that is to say, they offered to ameliorate misery and poverty while, at the same time, serving to further reformist illusions in the working people and to assuage the "guilty conscience" of upper and middle class Christians who felt the great contradiction between their evangelical words and their daily practice of religion. These Christians found comfort in the social doctrine of the church advocated by Catholic Action, or the Daughters of Mary, or the Gentlemen of the Most High.

This role of accomplice to the dictatorship changed during the 1970's under the double influence of a church that emerged from a rural and working class people, and because of the hierarchy's recent sensitivity to the injustices of the regime and to the almost universal protest which erupted especially after the earthquake of 1972.

As for the Protestant churches, the first to arrive was the Moravian Church on the Atlantic Coast (1847), which represented the ideological legitimation of British and later American penetration in the region. This church brought with it an imperial vision of life--elegant clothing, kitchen utensils, furniture, large houses with many conveniences--as well as a mode of thinking which socialized the indigenous peoples to pursue money in order to be able to acquire unnecessary possessions, and thus led to their proletarianization in the foreign companies that were established to develop wood, fish, rubber, gold, and banana resources.[39] While it never challenged the Yankee companies, the Moravian Church represented the only refuge, independent of the asphyxiating world of foreign companies, where social relationships could develop. Thus it attained a considerable influence.

Other Yankee missionaries arrived in Nicaragua in the period of Zelaya at the time of the North American imperialist expansion in the Caribbean that took possession of Spain's colonies, Cuba, the Dominican Republic, and Puerto Rico. These missionary congregations transplanted the dominant theology of the United States, which was spiritualistic, pietistic, puritan, and psychological in nature and unconcerned with the social problems of the exploited workers. In that way, the Protestants inculcated, together with the learning of English, an admiration

55

of the North American way of life, and, at the same time, transmitted[40] fears of Communism and of revolutionary thinking. "The Evangelical Church welcomed Somocismo and the work of the '...pacification of the Segovias.' Protestant leaders of great social influence guided the evangelical masses in support of Somocista liberalism... while although they were Puritan as far as the vices of alcohol and other evils, they progressively became accomplices in torture and the abuse of power."[41]

In the 1960's, in the "stage of the revolutionary ascent of the masses (1956-75)"[42] and in the period of the first guerrilla wave in Latin America, under the stimulus of the Cuban Revolution, Christians experienced a process of change that carried them in the 1970's into three different models of the "Church," each attached politically to a different persuasion: 1) a reformist model which became the opposition bourgeoisie, Democratic Liberation Union - Broad Opposition Front (UDEL-FAO); 2) a reactionary model, supportive of the dictatorship; and 3) a Christian liberating sector tied to the revolutionary bloc -- the Sandinista Front for National Liberation (FSLN), The United Peoples Movement (MPU), The Twelve (los Doce), and the National Patriotic Front (FPN).[43] In summary, the religious institutions in Nicaragua served historically, with few exceptions in the last decade, as an ideological legitimator of the Somocista society by means of the transmission of a series of beliefs, concepts, and practices such as:

Passivity: God is the only motor of all the changes and events that occur in reality. Man is impotent on his own; only with prayers and pleas to God will the rains come, will the corn flourish, and will we liberate ourselves from our oppressors.

Resignation: Against violence and exploitation it is necessary to turn the other cheek, to forgive, and to suffer in order to be compensated after death. Death and suffering are raised to the status of virtues, inasmuch as one must accept the "tests" that God has sent us.

Ritualism: The authentic Christian is the one who fulfills the liturgical formalities; that is to say, he always goes to mass, he prays and strikes his chest, and he is generous with alms to the needy and contributions to the parish.

Apoliticism: Religion has nothing to do with politics, inasmuch as its interest is merely spiritual, and the most important thing for the human being is his spiritual development; that is, religious development. The Christian defense of the poor does not refer to the poor as a social class, but to the poor in spirit.

56

Ultraterrestrial: The Reign of God does not constitute itself in this world, but it is after death that we will find justice, peace, and abundance.

Moralism: Social problems are due to sin, to evil, to the vices of individual people. The solution is in repentance and the conversion of conscience.

Idealism: An abstract, deductive, and metaphysical theology predominates. We talk about man as a generic being, with an ahistoric human nature. History can be explained as a fight between good and evil, between sinners and the righteous.

Intimacy: One represents Christianity as a state of internal animation, a charisma that expresses itself in a special individual relationship between the believer and God, a bond between God and man without the mediation of other men.

Submission: The institutional structure, especially the Catholic one, develops submissive obedience before the authorities through their hierachical organization that reproduces the model which existed under European feudalism for various centuries when the Catholic Church was a major force. To disobey a priest or even a bishop is to disobey God since they are His voices on Earth.

Clericalism: The Church is based upon the leadership of professional clergy. The lay believers have only a subordinate and passive role in the interpretation of doctrine or in liturgical practices.

Conclusions

We see that the dominant ideology during the Somoza period was reproduced through different channels, of which the religious institutions were more important than the means of mass communication, the educational apparatus, or the family. The other institutions for the transmission of ideology -- such as political parties, businesses, guilds, unions, and social clubs -- had less importance than the four institutions considered in this section. Nevertheless, they all contributed to forming a coherent system of values, beliefs, and concepts that we can characterize briefly by the following characteristics, which are not a complete scientific definition, but a rough approximation.

Idealism: Man appears as an abstract being. His essence is ideas which are the true motors of historical change. Individual or social conscience determines the political and economic relationships of a society.

Fatalism: The social order, like the natural order, is not an historical product of human activity, but an eternal system, unchangeable -- a product of Destiny, God, or Nature. The differences between men and classes are something natural and logical, as there are differences among minerals and animals, angels and archangels.

Liberalism: One cannot put restrictions on the individual freedom of people to consume, to express themselves, to produce, or to do business. Those who do not have the economic flexibility to exercise all of these individual freedoms should save and work with eagerness to be able to "climb socially." Democracy is defined as an electoral system based upon competition at regular intervals between political parties for government positions.

Pro-Capitalism: The private ownership of the means of production is a natural or divine and inalienable right. Thanks to the interest and industrious quality of capitalists for increasing production and bettering techniques, the entire society benefits from the free competition between them. The underdeveloped countries will arrive at the state of material well-being of the more advanced societies like the United States if they allow the penetration of capital, technology, incentives, and work methods.

Anticommunism: With the alleged promise of bettering the working class, a bureaucratic elite (the Communist Party or C.P.) has set up a series of totalitarian states. The C.P. takes all freedom from men and maintains itself in power by means of repression while trying to take over the whole globe (Russian imperialism). The North American "doctrine of national security" puts forth this vision of a bipolar world where Nicaraguans are a part of Western and Christian civilization together with the United States.

Competition: As with animals, the fight between individuals of the same species serves to guarantee the elimination of the less able. Thus, in human society, competition is necessary to perfect ourselves, although this implies the suffering and disappearance of more backward peoples, classes, or individuals.

Individualism: Everyone should look out for himself without relying on others for help. Freedom is understood as the unrestricted possibility for all people to achieve that which they want and are able to possess. Social classes do not exist, but rather individuals with different ways of thinking and behaving.

Consumerism: The goal of human happiness is to reach material well-being, thanks to the possession of a large quantity of material goods. Thus, in the United States, where individuals have so many possessions, the people are all of the middle class, live happily, and are free and civilized.

Racism: Biologically superior races exist, as much physically as mentally; in respect to others, the white race is superior to the black or Indian. The mixed races, such as the mestizos or mulattos do not achieve the superiority of the white race. The superior are more able to do intellectual tasks than the inferior, to whom manual labor corresponds. The backwardness of some countries is due to traits such as laziness, indolence, violence, and vices. The solution is to be found in imitating and intermarrying with the superior races.

Machismo: To the man corresponds the role of head of the family; to the woman, the subordinate role, as well as the hardest and most routine tasks of domestic work. The woman is temperamentally weak.

Fate: The things that happen in life are matters of luck, of chance. Some have the fortune of being born intelligent and rich, while others have to wait for "destiny" or "God" to reward them in a miraculous and fortuitous way, as with the lottery.

These concepts that we have mentioned comprise an interrelated and coherent set of beliefs that served objectively to legitimate the political dicta- torial system of Somoza and to maintain the social relationships of economic production in the "old" Nicaragua dependent on imperialism. This system ended on July 19, 1979, with the triumph of the insurrection led by the FSLN. Since then a new historical stage has opened up, which "doesn't deal with a simple change of leaders but rather a change in structure" (Carlos Fonseca). In other words, we see now the disarticulation of the economic, political, and ideological structures of the past as part of the construction of the New Society.

THE PERPETUATION OF BOURGEOIS IDEOLOGY IN THE SANDINISTA REVOLUTION

The taking of political power on July 19, 1979, meant the disintegration of the Somocista state, and the initiation of a new state based upon the fundamen- tal interests of the workers and peasants which takes into consideration the interests of other patriotic sectors which participated in the beginnings of a mixed economy and political pluralism. This structur- al change signified radical change in the ideological apparatuses which had the greatest dependency on state power -- the school system and the mass media -- and to a lesser degree, even in the institutions that possessed some relative autonomy from the power of the state, such as religious institutions and the family.

Without a doubt, political military changes have proceeded more rapidly than ideological changes, which are permeated with the heavy inheritance of the past. Our vanguard (The FSLN) stated: "The most difficult task is to conquer the bourgeois ideology that has penetrated the people. Revolutionaries can take economic power with relative ease, but what is most difficult is to take hold of the ideological power of that society; the intangible power that is expressed in the mentality of men."

Notwithstanding this difficulty in the nascent revolutionary process, the advances in the fields of education, culture, and mass communications have been substantial in only three years since the revolution. In a summary way, we will point out these changes so that later we may more easily discuss our principal theme: the transformation of religious institutions from the privileged ideological channels of the middle classes.

The School System

We can summarize the quantitative and qualitative advances in education by the following:

-The National Literacy Campaign (CNA) reduced the illiteracy rate from 52% to 12.9% in the population over 10 years of age, mobilizing close to 100,000 youths who succeeded in understanding the peasant's reality, surmounting in this way both the old prejudices against the "barbarity" and "lack of culture" of the Indian-peasant, and their own prejudices against rural manual labor. The youths converted themselves into teachers of adults and, at the same time, apprentices of the peasants in learning their way of life. This collective and participatory method of education of the CNA hastened the transformation of traditional teaching methods and teacher/student relationships in the schools and colleges where these youthful literacy volunteers were educated.

-Literacy in Misquito-Sumo-English languages was achieved by 12,664 inhabitants of the Atlantic Coast. This program was intended to contribute to the betterment of the less appreciated ethnic groups and to the

---

*Bayardo Arce has emphasized this position most forcefully in "Por Una Cultura Revolucionaria," Barricada; February 20, 1980.

national integration of these people, besides allowing for the restoration of their culture.

-Adult education that has continued since the CNA means daily participation, for about 2 hours, of 163,355 people (1982) in 18,692 Popular Education Collectives where they learn together, by means of a pedagogy that flows from their own reality, in order to help them understand their own lives, and be able to change them, under the direction of "people's teachers" who are their peers.

-Enrollment in preschool education increased from 9,000 children attending in 1978 to 41,215 in 1982, by means of 13 pilot centers and 370 rooms annexed to primary schools, where from an early age children learn in a collective and cooperative manner to master everyday activities (dressing, eating, playing, knowing).

-Advances in Primary Education have almost doubled the number of children who attended school during the Somoza period, so that today, of every 100 children between 7 and 12 years of age, some 80 attend primary school. Also, in Middle School Education, we observed an increase from 99,000 students in 1978 to 151,000 today. At the University level, the number of matriculating students in 1982 increased by 92.1% over 1976, with an increase of 200% in state aid per student.

-In rural technical education, four institutes have been reactivated, and another three have been created and supplied with machinery, implements, and qualified technicians.

-Seven normal schools have been created; these were added to the five that already existed, with the goal of graduating some 700 primary teachers annually to fill the large shortage; presently Cuban teachers are helping us.

-A Department of Special Education, created for handicapped children, is in charge of 26 special education centers in the country.

-The Program for the Promotion of Communal Educational Development has taken charge of establishing school, family, and communal vegetable gardens; carpentry and sewing workshops; and rural work-study schools.

-Thirty-eight libraries have been equipped, mobile libraries have been organized, and a national annual campaign to improve the libraries has begun.

-Work study activities permit the participation of more than 120,000 youths in harvest activities, reforestation, and environmental improvement, thus encouraging an appreciation of manual labor and a contribution by students to the economic reconstruction of the country.

-The National Educational Consultation has served as a democratic mechanism for popular discussion of the future educational policies of the government. Some 30 organizations and nearly 50,000 people have participated.[44]

-Other achievements to be noted are the increase in the number of schools constructed even in the most remote regions of the country, the scholarship program for students of limited resources, and the agreements with friendly countries to give scholarships to nearly 1,000 university students. The educational work carried out by the Mass Organizations, by the Unidades de Capacitación del Estado, by the National System for Professional Development, by the Nicaraguan Institute of Public Administration, or by centers dedicated to Popular Education like the Center for Agrarian Education and Promotion (CEPA), must be mentioned also.

But what is most important to realize is not the numbers but the qualitative jump that the numbers imply and that defy measurement; that is, the advancement of awareness, or creative and critical skills, and of participation and organization of large sectors of the population. That is what is essential in this data: forty percent of the population of Nicaragua currently participates in some type of education.[45]

That does not mean that there are still not obstacles that need to be overcome, such as the need to change from a traditional teaching-learning methodology to one which is both theoretical and practical, participatory and critical. Nicaragua is searching for a methodology which can grasp the contributions of the Literacy Campaign (CNA), of Adult Education, and of the Latin American experience of consciousness-raising education without falling into the easy tendency of copying models which have already been surpassed by Nicaragua's own revolutionary process.

The Artistic-Cultural System

Without doubt the stimulus given to artistic cultural creativity by the Government of National Reconstruction and the Popular Organizations is shaping a new strong ideology of the people, which barely existed in the Somoza period and was overshadowed by elite dominance of the means of communication. If we consider that, in the first place, in the previous era, "popular culture was repressed, and that on it were imposed the colonizing values of the middle class, then we have two tasks ahead of us; to liberate our culture and to purify it. . .a culture to create the New Man. . .a culture to change reality. . .a

62

revolutionary democratic[46] popular, national and anti-imperialist culture."[46]

The insurrection was the first step in a great cultural process. Even going to the theater, the people became aware of themselves. Slogans were painted on the walls. Poetry was epigrammatic and political, and craftsmanship could be seen in homemade bombs. "We have rediscovered the agitative power of folklore, of what is ours, of the word 'Nicaragua'. All art, imagination, and culture are means to obtain the triumph over the dictatorship.[47] It is, in a way, an ascent of imagination to power."[47]

Among the most notable advances we must point out was the creation of the Council of Popular Culture, which organized 24 Centers where poetry, theatre, art, and music (140 workshops) were encouraged, as well as 27 expositions of handicrafts and plastic arts which emulated native art. These expositions were organized simultaneously with development programs for artisans. Also, we must mention the establishment of a national theatre; the production of 30 films and their distribution through the "Travelling Theatre" to impoverished areas; the promotion of 114 national and international artistic gala events; the production of over 100,000 texts of more than 30 different titles; fairs for the rescue and promotion of culture such as the Piñata and the Festival of Corn; the development of a network of public libraries and travelling libraries; the opening of different museums and the remodeling of those that were previously established. The government also sponsored Nicaraguan artistic groups in their travels to other nations on more than 312 occasions.

In this enormous task of the creation of an authentic popular culture, the Ministry of Culture, the Sandinista Youth Organization, and other groups such as the Movement for Agrarian Expression have undertaken a tremendous responsibility.

The intellectuals and artists who are forged in the heat of this revolutionary process are no longer an elite which turns its back on its country and its people. Rather than copy foreign models, "the Nicaraguan intellectual ought to be the motivating center of Latin American intellectuals. They ought to organize themselves and their ideas in order that they acquire a tangible and irrepressible force among the peoples . . . . The ideas of peace, the ideas of liberation and social justice ought to become material force among the peoples of America . . . ."[48]

Now the intellectuals and artists are part of the same working class nation which is recovering and developing the creative potential which had been suffocated by the injustices of the Somoza period.

Now artists are well-rounded revolutionaries. That is to say, they are members of the militia, literacy volunteers, and health workers. Now it is not a question of maintaining a separation between manual work and intellectual work, but of developing both in harmony. Besides, as has been made clear in the recent debate about the function of the artist in the revolution, it is not a question of "all creative expression must be political expression," or that art must limit itself to "the expression of the profoundest sentiments of the human being." It is a question of respecting the full and multifaceted human experience which cannot be reduced to a crude, simplistic realism nor to an intimate subjectivism. Perhaps in the artistic peasants of MESCATE we can find a model of the popular artist and also the resolution of this dichotomy. Because of their social position and their creative capacity, it falls to them naturally to "learn from the masses in order to be able to educate the masses" (Carlos Fonseca); and their art--without possessing the technical qualitites of a professional--possesses the force which comes from its being the revolutionary art of the people and not simply art for the people.

In conclusion, the Sandinista Revolution has created an ideological structure which has undermined bourgeois pseudo-culture intended for mass-market consumption (novels, magazines, sexist or violent movies) and has established the bases for a new culture, rooted in the culture of "protests and denunciations" of the insurrectionary period and carried out by the same people who are awakening from their lethargy to exericse their creativity and imagination, as much in art as in economics and defense. Nicaragua's culture is attempting to purify itself from bourgeois tendencies and go forth with an ideology based on cooperation, solidarity, good humor, modesty, and uncompromising commitment to liberation for the people of Latin America.

The Mass Media (MCM)

After the triumph, the restrictive radio and television laws, known as "The Black Code" (Código Negro), were abolished and replaced by the Law of Mass Communications (August 1979), which stated that "freedom of information is one of the fundamental principles of an authentic democracy and the State must guarantee that no purposeful possibility exists to subject it, directly or indirectly, to the economic power of any social group for the purpose of guaranteeing its full independence . . . ." This law embodies the principles established in the Statute of Rights and Guarantees of the Citizen, the fundamental law of the National Government of Reconstruction.

Also, the freedom to form unions under the Popular Sandinista Revolution permitted the rise of the Journalists' Union of Nicaragua (UPN), which is the major union of journalists and workers in the field of communication. A very small group has remained in the Association of Journalists of Nicaragua (APN), aligned with the Democratic Coordinating Group, which represents the opposing middle class. If we examine the newspapers, we see that there are three that are nationwide: Barricada, the official organ of the FSLN; El Nuevo Diario which, although independent, has a policy of supporting the revolution; and La Prensa, which is opposed to the revolutionary process. The open opposition of this newspaper to the Revolution, which on innumerable occasions has bordered on calumny and insult, is a clear example of the freedom of expression that exists in this country.[49]

In the area of broadcasting, there are 51 radio stations, of which 34 are privately owned and the rest state-controlled. In the area of television, the two existing channels are public. The intention of the middle class to start a private TV channel gave rise to a debate which focused on state control of the MCM. Two different concepts of freedom of expression clearly emerged: on the one hand, there is the bourgeois view that holds that there should be no restriction on individual freedom; on the other hand, a popular concept of freedom maintained that the individual's interests can be subordinated to the interests of society.

The detractors of state regulation of the MCM forget the nature of the new revolutionary state as an expression of the interests of the people in the first place.

"Those who exercise control over this public system are the representatives of the Revolutionary State, the Organization of the Masses and the FSLN, an expression of the best of our people. Those who exercise control over the private means of communication are the owners and their announcers. For this reason the National Government of Reconstruciton denied a permit for the installation of a private TV channel. Is it possible perhaps that we are unaware of who has the capital and the international connections to install an expensive TV channel?"[50]

The middle class which utilized the Somoza state to hold on to its privileges, complains about the state's intervention in favor of the majority, and proclaims itself "the genuine representative of the people" and confuses the pretense of its own interests with those of the working class. The emphasis given by the RPS on systematic and objective reporting of national and international news has been a decisive step toward the democratization of Nicaraguan society, as well as a step toward public awareness, since being informed is an indispensable requisite for conscientious participation in the political decisions of government.

Since the escalated aggression of imperialism which followed the electoral triumph of Ronald Reagan, an ideologically united opposition has unleashed an orchestrated and scientific campaign of confusion. By utilizing subliminal and sophisticated methods of associating images and values, they have attempted to again create the climate of uncertainty and fear such as that brought about by the CIA before the fall of Allende in Chile and before the electoral defeat of Michael Manley in Jamaica.[51]

For these reasons, laws were decreed which prohibited the dissemination of news that might cause speculation in prices and goods, or that deal with national security matters without prior consultation with corresponding state agencies (Decrees Nos. 511, 512, 513). Later, when a state of emergency was declared in March 1982 because of the imminent threat of counterrevolutionary military invasion, prior censorship of all MCM news was implemented, and sanctions were established for those who distort or falsify the news in such a way as to endanger peace and national security. The suspensions decreed against several reactionary media institutions have been in answer to violations of these laws; obviously, the middle class have taken a position of provocation and confrontation with the precise objective of having their media outlets closed or suspended. This serves their purposes of presenting themselves, to the international press, as victims of "Sandinist- communist totalitarianism."

In summary, a great deal still has to be done by the MCM, especially regarding several North American TV broadcasts, movies, and scandal sheets that may serve to revive middle class ideology. But the progress made in only three years of revolution is enormous also -- especially advances in access to information and in the fostering of new values. For example, the Sandinista government has prohibited the use of the female body as an object to be exploited in advertisements and has banned both the advertisement

of alcoholic beverages and tobacco on television and the commercial use of Christmas religious festivals to sell products. Regarding freedom of expression, a new concept of freedom has evolved in contrast to that of the middle class, and the new concept subordinates the rights of the individual to the needs and interests of society. Also, one must realize that the presence of counterrevolutionary threats and intervention have brought about a wartime situation which, in turn, has limited public expression that might directly or indirectly aid the enemy who has regularly penetrated Nicaraguan borders and massed troops a few kilometers from Nicaragua.

The Family

Clearly, the transformations in family relations which have taken place do not compare with those accomplished in the fields of education, culture, or the mass media. The leaders of the revolution lacked mechanisms to transmit their desires for new family values into the heart of the family. Further, they said, "we have to honorably admit that we have not confronted with the same courage or decisiveness, the struggle for the liberation of women."[52] Nevertheless, in the third year of the revolution, significant advances in family relations had taken place because of the following factors:

On a juridical level, the Statute on Rights and Guarantees has already established norms that mark a clear break from previous legislation. Under the Sandinista government, the following principles prevail:

a) The equality of rights and responsibilities among men and women in the home (Art. 34).
b) The mutual duties of parents and children in assistance and nurture (Art. 34).
c) Equality among "legitimate" children and those born out of wedlock (Arto. 34).
d) The prohibition of employment harmful to children.
e) Maternity protection before and after giving birth.

These measures have been brought about in conjunction with other laws, such as the Social Security law, which protects the pregnant woman and her children; the Law of Accountability between Father, Mother, and Children, which spells out the principles of shared responsibilities, mutual cooperation, and equality between the spouses; the law that regulates payments in agriculture courts (attempting to avoid salary discrimination against women and children); the law regulating domestic work (housecleaning), which attempts to do away with excessively long work days and overexploitation; the law that prohibits the female body to be used in commercial advertising; and the recently planned Food Law, which attempts to make operative mutual family obligations regarding a person's basic nutritional needs.

But more important than legal regulations are actions and deeds that have brought about a practical transformation in family relations. Among other things, the new family was forged in the insurrection, which produced the embryo of relationships which after the victory became dominant. Specifically, the revolutionary process brought about a qualitative change in the roles of women and children.

> "The daily activities of women were in marked contrast to the social habits that women had practiced before the war. The concept of fatherland even replaced for many women the concept of maternity as a catalyst for action; working together politically made women realize how isolating domestic work was, took them out of the home, and united them into a social force . . . women have become creators, not subjects, of history"[53]

In short, we can observe that since the Triumph different processes have developed which have left the imprint of important changes in values, beliefs, and practices within the family:

-The National Literacy Campaign (CNA) has changed children and adolescents into teachers of literacy and also into students and members of farm and worker families. Young people matured quickly and broke with their traditional passivity and dependence. Their motives ceased to be based simply on the latest fad or banality or drugs. In the revolution they found a fertile field to cultivate their ideals of fraternity and love. Moreover, the CNA permitted women to participate in activities which were previously unknown in their traditional roles as housewives.

-The expansion of Mass Organizations, especially the Nicaraguan Women's Association (AMLAE) and the Sandinista Defense Committees (CDS), oriented the family toward tasks of a national or communal nature. The organizations completed an important job of education in new Sandinista values through sacrifice and work for common good and through cultural activities and political mobilization. Participation in revolutionary vigilance, in the voluntary police

force, and in the militia has resulted in a social-
ization to values such as the defense of the nation or
the safety of one's neighborhood. It is no longer a
matter of just looking out for one's family, but
rather one of being concerned with all the families of
the country and with the future of Nicaragua's people.
Thus, the family loses exclusivity but gains collective solidarity.

-The health campaigns, especially the
mother-child programs, the transfer of land under both
agrarian and urban reform laws, and other advances in
the purchasing power of the people have brought about
security and tranquility which did not exist in the
Somoza era. This has had an impact on family life,
where there is now less tension, fewer infant deaths,
and more happiness and peace.

-A large number of educational programs have
been instituted in the process of changing family
relations. These include the Quincho Barrilete
program; special education for children with discipline problems; and Centers for Pre-school Development, which, while consolidating education and
nutrition programs for children, also permit the
involvement of women in educational tasks far removed
from routine chores of the home. Other programs have
been developed by the Ministry of Education (MED) for
parents of school children, by the Nicaraguan Women's
Association (AMNLAE) for political and ideological
training, by the Ministry of Agriculture and Agrarian
Reform (MINDINRA) and The Ministry of Health (MINSA)
for the preparation of a balanced diet, and by the
Sandinista Television Network (SSTV), radio, and
pamphlets for the discussion of topics such as child
care or sewing. One must also mention the re-education programs for prostitutes and criminals which have
won international attention.

In summary, much still remains to be done in the
conversion of the family as a vehicle for the propagation of a new set of values. There still are many
so-called revolutionaries who do not go beyond preaching against male chauvinism, against the separation of
the sexes in the workplace, or against the exploitation of domestic workers, just as there are many women
who passively accept masculine domination. Nevertheless, if we compare the present situation, not with
the ideal future one, but with the conditions of the
recent and real past which exist even today in neigh-
boring countries, we see that progress has been
considerable in only three years of revolution. This
is especially true if we take into consideration the
burdensome ideological inheritance of the past and the
tests imposed by the development of our economy.

Revolutionary Ideology

The revolutionary ideology transmitted by the educational and cultural systems, the MCM, and the Mass Organizations has attempted to bring about values such as cooperation, solidarity, altruism, austerity, humility, and an appreciation for manual labor -- values that are rooted in Sandinista principles and that are forged daily, not only in conversations and speeches, but also in actions.

This ideology is of necessity original because it is the product of the specific social praxis of Nicaragua's revolutionary process, which rescues the best of Nicaragua's past and fuses it with creative and revolutionary practices of the present, in combination with the scientific concepts and contributions of worldwide revolutionary thought. The libertarian rebellion of Nicarao and the natives who fought against Spanish oppression joined with the class pride of Augusto C. Sandino, who stated, "My greatest honor is to arise from the bosom of the oppressed . . . proud that in my veins flows, more than any other, the blood of the American Indian."[54] This ideological inheritance is strengthened by the work of the FSLN, which believes "a Sandinista possesses above all a lack of pretense . . . . The Sandinista knows how to help his companions recognize his shortcomings and frailties."[55]. The qualities of a revolutionary are his simplicity, his frankness, his loyalty, and his sacrifice for the liberation of his people, since "a Sandinista is one who is more concerned for the people than for himself."[56]

In contrast to the ideological views which prevailed under the Somoza regime, we maintain that: a) history is not idealistic, but empirical since it is "the individual who determines the social conscience" and not vice versa; b) in opposition to fatalism, we believe in the active and conscious participation of "a people as master of its history and architect of its freedom" (FSLN anthem); c) in contrast to capitalist liberalism, what has occurred in Nicaragua was a real liberation based on the termination of economic exploitation and on the development of productive forces: Individual freedom was subordinated to the collective interest; d) in answer to capitalist rationalizations, the working class proclaims its defense of the revolution "for the construction of socialism," a socialism appropriate to national reality; e) in answer to anticommunism and the bipolar vision of the world which places us within "Western Civilization," the revolutionary government is part of the Movement of Non-Aligned Countries and advocates peaceful coexistence, self-determination, and international solidarity with peoples who fight for their liberation from imperialism, racism, Zionism, and apartheid; and f) as opposed to bourgeois democracy, we move toward real popular democracy based on "the involvement of the masses in all aspects of social life."[57]

This revolutionary ideology has gestated in the hard struggle against bourgeois ideology which continued its propaganada in the interior of the country through the penetration of the pro-imperialist MCM of Central America, using well-planned tactics involving counterrevolutionary gossip and humor, and by means of religious institutions, the central theme in this paper.

The Religious Institutions

The transmission of bourgeois and imperialist ideology through Nicaragua's religious institutions began a few days after the revolutionary victory with the Letter of the Episcopal Conference of Nicaragua (CEN), in which a number of concerns and fears were expressed: the "slow down of judicial proceedings, lack of freedom of expression, . . . would threaten the confidence held by interested parties in revolutionary projects . . . . There exist anomalies such as illegal procedures against private property and arbitrary imprisonment."[58]

Nicaraguans themselves asked, who was fearful when the National Guard and the ominous dictatorship had just been expelled? Who could suffer anguish because of the confiscation of the wealth of Somoza's followers? No doubt it was not the populace who jubiliantly, although in a disorganized manner in those first days, overturned a situation of centuries of exploitation. Those fears were expressed by Monsignor Miguel Obando y Bravo (MOB) on July 17 when he tried to intervene and enlarge the membership in the governing junta for the purpose of neutralizing "the radical elements." That is to say, they were the fears of the middle-class opposition which desired a reform, not a revolution, of the old order: Somocizmo without Somoza.

In response to the letter of the CEN, the Junta of the National Government of Reconstruction requested a dialogue with them and called upon four priests to take ministerial posts. Also, the clergy's participation in the Council of State, which was set to begin the following year, was welcomed. The next letter of the CEN in November 1979 represented without a doubt the closest rapprochement and understanding between the Catholic hierarchy and the National Reconstruction

71

Government (GRN). Yet in this communication there appeared certain viewpoints of the middle class: for example, the bishops said, "Many forces have contributed generously to our historical process and no one should impede their future contribution" and "Many Nicaraguans are fearful now." Similar thoughts were expressed by the Superior Council of Private Enterprise (COSEP) in a similar communication in which they lamented the fact that private enterprise did not have more participation in the affairs of state and in the handling of the economy.

In 1980 when the whole nation was preparing for the National Literacy Crusade (CNA), several religious sectors denounced "The imminent Cubanization of Nicaragua," referring to the presence of 1,200 Cuban teachers out of a total of 90,000 literacy teachers! As a special contribution to the literacy campaign, the Episcopal Conference of Latin America (CELAM) -- (a body that before the triumph never denounced the atrocities of the Somoza regime, but since July 11, 1979, was worried about the possible fall of the Sandinista government to communism) -- sent, with the consent of the CEN, catechism manuals to each diocese. The manuals were denounced by the basic Christian communities (CEBs), comprised of farmers and workers, which considered the manuals "irrelevant and unrelated to the social aspects of daily life."[59]

Before the beginning of this campaign, unleashed through the opposition mass media and by certain religious sectors, committed Christians -- Protestants as well as Catholics -- declared publicly in a document dated March 20, 1980, "that on this day members of the counter-revolutionary right of Nicaragua raised the flag of private enterprise, of political pluralism and of classless nationalism which they attributed to Sandino at the same time that they proclaimed their decision to fight for religious freedom." At that moment, one already saw clearly the strategem of the middle class, which was also noted by Philip Agee as a sure tactic of the Central Intelligence Agency (CIA) to undermine the Sandinista victory, although the extent of this ideological offense was minimal at that point compared to the present.[60] A few weeks later, in May 1980, on the critical occasion during which there was 1) the resignation of Alfonso Robelo, Violeta Chamorro, and several state officials, 2) a conflict between the employees and the manager of La Prensa, and 3) the installation of the Council of State with a clear majority representing people's organizations, the CEN requested the dismissal of two priests from the Council of State and declared that "the delegation of the Association of Nicaraguan

Clergy (ACLEN) represent[ed] only said association and not the church as such."[61]

On an international level, the Archbishop of Mexico distributed a report dated May 5, 1980, to all parishes in the country, referring specifically to Nicaragua, stating that: "Everything indicates that the present trend will culminate through gradual entrenchment into a regime with definite communist characteristics, under strong Cuban influence . . . . There are already signs that there is an intent to discredit the Church and religion."[62]

This explains the interest of the bourgeois opposition and their allies in the Catholic hierarchy in having the priests resign from government posts. After all, not only were the priests in government providing the revolution with badly needed technical and professional assistance, but also their involvement was of great significance in terms of the internal and international image it was creating. This also explains middle-class opposition to the Council of State for not having given them control of the majority of seats they had requested and their boycott of the legislative body that symbolized national unity, political pluralism, and true democratization of the revolutionary political system. These moves also found their echo in the Nicaraguan Bishops Council (CEN). At the same time, the international campaign of calumny against the revolution had already begun, as in the case of the Archbishop of Mexico. This campaign was fortified through the willingness of major news agencies, which control 80% of world news broadcasting, to spread this slander to the rest of the world.

But this was only the beginning of the utilization of religious institutions by the pro-imperialist middle class. After the May crisis, the opposition's ideological expression was sharpened in ecclesiastical circles by means of a charismatic movement, short courses on Christianity, the creation of Christian Parents Associations, the formation of a Center for Religious Studies (CER) as a transmitter of a medieval theology, and the utilization of processions and popular acts of religiosity such as the Coronation of the Virgin (Aug. 15, 1980). The archbishop invited the president of Costa Rica and a large delegation to this ceremony without informing the authorities. In this ceremony, sponsored by members of the middle class, the leaders of the Nicaraguan government were hissed at upon arrival, while Obando made reference to "the monster with seven heads that hovers over our country threatening its freedoms" in a clear metaphor of the alleged totalitarian communist movement that threatened Nicaragua.

At the same time, the opposition parties jointly demanded the rapid promulgation of the law of political parties and of elections as "the only way of guaranteeing a truly democratic revolution." This period was also marked by the first utilization of anticommunism by followers of Somoza from the Atlantic Coast. This took place in the form of a demonstration against international volunteers from Cuba and the government in Bluefields (Sept. 30, 1980). It was at that time that Mons. Obando defined the "Democratic State" as one in which there are "well-organized elections, different political parties and popular participation, but one should not exaggerate the will of the majority, because it can change into mass democracy and the masses are the chief enemy of democracy."

In response to the demands of middle class opponents, the government set 1985 as the year for elections and defined democracy as "the participation of the masses in all aspects of social life" (Aug. 23, 1980). Some days later (Sept. 7, 1980), the FSLN published its declaration on religion, in which it guaranteed freedom for all religious cults, permitted Christians to participate in politics, denied that the FSLN was attempting to divide the church, and indicated that while the state was secular, it was not incompatible for one to be both a believer and a revolutionary. The response of the CEN (Oct. 10, 1980) reiterated the principal complaints of the middle class against the government in suggestive and metaphorical language.

What were these insinuations? Let us look at the texts: "No one can arrogate to himself the right to govern or be aided by foreign forces nor can he [arrogate to himself] the role of representative; in such a case, we would not be any better off than in the past era." That is to say, the Episcopal Conference repeated the accusation that the FSLN was a military party, which depended on force and on Cuban support to impose itself on the people without being elected, establishing a dictatorship similiar to that of the Somoza regime. Also, the bishops reiterated the constant complaint of the middle class that "the army should not be labeled 'Sandinista'" because the armed forces should serve the whole nation and not a political party like the FSLN. How simplistic -- to pretend that crimes are apolitical when the National Guard always served to guarantee private ownership of the means of production!

For greater clarity, another paragraph stated that "Nicaragua has set forth in search of her historical liberation, not a new Pharaoh." And it cautioned that an army without public support degenerates into an army of occupation. On the other hand, the Catholic bishops felt that the lay character of the state would give advantage to those who had no faith, suggesting tactically that the state should adopt a religion (as was done by Emperor Constantine or the Spanish Kings or the Conservatives in Nicaragua a century ago). A little further on, they dealt with the theme of religious participation in state affairs, saying that "Totalitarian regimes, because of their materialistic philosophy, deny to the church any meaningful participation in the national economy. But [they] strategically accept instrumental participation. This is another way to subtly convert the church into an instrument."[63] Here they compared the GRN to a totalitarian system, extrapolating the historic experiences of other revolutions, in which, because of a lack of believers who were also revolutionaries as in Nicaragua, the treatment of religion had a solution quite different than that authorized by the Nicaraguan government and the FSLN. Moreover, the bishops were acting as if the Church still had the economic power which, in fact, the same liberal middle class had snatched from it in the time of José Santos Zelaya eighty years previously; they also forgot that for the FSLN religion was not necessarily "the opium of the people," even though they accused the FSLN of manipulating the Catholic church.

A few days later (Oct. 22, 1980), the same CEN came out with another pastoral letter entitled "Jesus Christ and the Unity of His Church in Nicaragua," in which the following were considered priority problems of the people: 1) "the offensive by materialistic ideologies," 2) family problems, and 3) doctrinal and moral confusion among ecclesiatical sectors. In this way the CEN expressed the fears of the middle class concerning changes in the family and in ideology in general. They were worried in particular about: 1) the growth of scientific understanding which exposed the social mechanisms of exploitation; 2) the growing commitment of youth to the transformation of society and the creation of new values of commitment to and solidarity with the poor; 3) the participation of clergy and laypersons in the tasks of consolidating the revolutionary process (health, education, people's organizations); and 4) clerical involvement in organizing basic Christian communities (CEBs), with an interpretation of the Gospel from the perspective of the exploited, and with a re-evaluation of the role of the laity in the church.

The Catholic hierarchy defended the most simplistic type of idealism by stating that "Life is the result of one's thinking. All that we are is the result of our thoughts,"[64] and it opposed the efforts

75

of reconstruction of the GRN with the argument that
"There are individuals who expect everything from
civilization, from a planned economy, from material
goods, from the work ethic . . . . They do not await
a Redeemer from above, but rather one from below, a
human, who prepares man for a terrestrial paradise."[65]
On the other hand, the subject of the family had
become another main point in middle class ideology,
which emphasized "The right of parents to educate
their children according to their Christian convictions," an allusion to the purported materialistic
indoctrination imposed by the Ministry of Education
(MED).

The same Episcopal Letter emphasized obedience
to the hierarchy as a basic principle of unity, since
the bishops had received said power from Jesus Christ
Himself through his apostles. That is to say, while
the people expressed their faith through participation
in the CEBs and in thousands of acts of love for one's
fellow man (programs of literacy, health, housing,
etc.), the bishops emphasized traditional forms of
liturgical expression, such as the Sunday mass and the
processions to prevent the deviation of the populace
toward other social goals. And while the people
exercised their right to vote and express themselves
in decisions that affected their social lives, the
hierarchy demanded unconditional and submissive
obedience under penalty of canonical sanctions. This
position not only expressed the hierarchy's desire to
maintain its control and power over religion, but also
expressed the intention of the middle class. Middle-
class support for the common values of the "Nicaraguan
Family" such as religious belief, nationalism, and
customs was intended to deny the existence of different social classes and to deny the objective character
of the struggle of opposing classes which logically
became more acute with each tangible advance in the
construction of a "New Society." Thus, as important
segments of the middle class attempted to regain their
power over the people through mobilization, propaganda, and proselytizing through their mass media, the
Catholic hierarchy tried to hold its authority over
the people who, day by day, marched toward fuller
liberation.

In the crisis of November 1980, we again noted a
position of support for these opposition sectors by
the Catholic hierarchy. This crisis was brought about
by the frustrated mobilization of the National Democratic Movement (MDN) in Nandaime; by the death of the
vice president of COSEP, Jorge Salazar (upon discover-
ing an armed, anti-government conspiracy with the
participation of ex-National Guard personnel); and by
the withdrawal of opposition sectors in the Council of

State. For example, in the prayers for the dead in memory of Salazar, the bishops stated that he was "a promise, an authentic leader." In reference to the Bureau of State Security and to the government, they said: "God forgive them for they know not what they do and do it because they do not know." A few days later Mons. Obando once again insisted on the resignation of the priests in government and set a deadline of the end of the year.[66]

During the first months of 1981, with the ascent of Reagan to the presidency of the United States, an economic, political, military, and ideological offensive was unleashed. The attacks from Honduras were intensified, and the plots to assassinate leaders of the Sandinista Revolution also increased. Economic sabotage, the boycott of loans, the defamation of the Nicaraguan experience to the rest of the world, and the manipulation of ethnic differences among the peoples of the Atlantic Coast, were intensified.

In this difficult period, the identification of the middle classes with certain religious sectors became more evident. Thus, for example, when José Esteban González, leader of the opposition Social Christian Party and head of the Permanent Commission for Human Rights, returned from a trip during which he had spread false accusations about the people detained by the government, he was received with a popular demonstration, during which the participants expressed their repudiation of him with hisses and eggs. On being detained by the Sandinista police, González declared that "God had already warned Christians that we would be persecuted." He later received a visit from Mons. Obando, who hastily prayed "for justice" in Nicaragua. Simultaneously, the bishop of Chontales, Mons. Vega, asked, "[are] the people gaining sovereignty or are they going down the road of turbulence and social confusion, where the only beneficiaries will be new oligarchies controlled by internationalists who have no interests in the people?"[67]

This same prelate had stated in his pastoral plan of 1981, which reached all the dioceses, that the problem that affected Nicaragua was that "there always are a few who take control of the government by force and wish to subjugate the rest of the people." During this period, the CELAM plan for Nicaragua, which affected the entire public, was more ostensibly put into effect. Its contents were:

-to promote days of prayer for the fate of Nicaragua and to ask for financial contributions throughout all of Latin America,

-to send 18,000 pamphlets and 10,000 copies of the New Testament, and

-to send delegates to Nicaragua to give courses in theology.

This program involved a budget of $270,000, of which $34,250 was sent by the North American firm of Miller and Co.[68] Secretly, this plan for aid involved the removal from the country of foreign priests dedicated to the revolutionary process and the prohibition of the participation of priests or religious figures in any government positions, political parties, or popular organizations. The removal of priests or foreign religious figures, whether they were from the countryside or from important parishes, was accomplished slowly but inexorably. To date, there have been sixteen cases. As the Brazilian theologian, Fray Betto, stated: "This campaign of aid brought about by CELAM assumes that for Marxist political logic which is emerging in Nicaragua there is only one antidote, the Christian faith. Thus, faith in God reduces itself to mere political rationality and in the last instance, it ends up identifying Christian faith with middle class ideology."[69]

The accusations against popular organizations, especially against the so-called turbas ("mobs"), as the opposition calls the Sandinista Defense Committees, have become more clear and direct on the part of several religious groups. The logical outcome has been the prohibition of participation by believers in those "mobs" as a prerequisite for staying within the framework of the religious institution. Such is the case with Seventh Day Adventists, Jehovah's Witnesses, the Mormons, or even the Catholic Church itself in the diocese of Chontales.

Another tactic used by opposition sectors of the middle class, since the beginning of 1981, has been to exalt and promote miraculous phenomena, such as the well-known case of the Virgin of Cuapa, which occurred during the time of the North American boycott, and months later was repeated in the case of the "Virgin who perspires." In the first case, the apparition had appeared to a humble sacristan of the town of Cuapa, Bernardo Martínez. La Prensa became aware of this fact and publicized this event at this critical period. Massive processions to Cuapa were organized by the middle class and the Catholic hierarchy. In the meantime, rumors were spread that the Virgin had come to condemn the Sandinista regime. Attempts were made to bribe Bernardo on several occasions to declare that the Virgin opposed the revolution. In a subsequent investigation, the sacristan declared that "they have wanted to manipulate me; the Robelistas wished that I go with them; even the followers of Somoza tried to gain my confidence and used me politically...so that I might talk things against the revolution."[70]

The case of the "Virgin who perspires," which brought about a wave of apparitions in candles and fires, was popularized by La Prensa at the moment when the people were mobilizing to repudiate the assassination of a Cuban teacher by bands of Somocistas. Subsequent investigation proved that the owner of the virgin was a delinquent with a long history and that the plaster statue had been set on a water fountain and then frozen. This was the reason that the "perspiration miracle" occurred. The archbishop himself had blessed the statue, and his supporters in the middle classes had organized processions to start a cult.

Against these repeated maneuvers, which were intended to take the public's attention away from the imperialist attacks, the government decreed that before any publication of any miracle could take place it had to be approved by the proper church authorities. The ultimate in bourgeois cynicism was the response to this governmental measure which claimed this directive was an act of interference and an attempt to weaken the validity of worship.[71]

In May 1981, the National Forum was initiated for the purpose of holding political debates among the political parties in order to promote national unity upon a pluralistic political base. The middle classes proposed that Mons. Obando take the role of mediator in this forum; this request was rejected by the Patriotic Front since the Catholic hierarchy itself had indicated its apolitical character. Furthermore, if one wanted to nominate a mediator, the potential candidate would have to be impartial. Obando was clearly identified with the opposition political parties.

A few days later (January 6, 1981), the Episcopal Conference issued a strong communiqué calling for the immediate resignation of the priests in government posts, under the threat of sanctions provided by the laws of the church. At the same time, the Episcopal Conference attacked the Historical Institute, the Valdivieso Center, and the Center for Agrarian Education and Promotion (CEPA) -- organizations with a clear Christian commitment to the liberation of the Nicaraguan people. Immediately after this Communiqué, Mons. Obando and other bishops went to Rome to meet with Vatican authorities, Central American religious leaders, and CELAM, for the purpose of guaranteeing their support and accelerating the removal of all foreign religious figures from the country. This trip was used by Mons. Obando in order to make a series of defamatory statements, such as the following, to the outside world: "After two years of the revolution our country has fallen into Marxism under the Cuban model"; "Nicaragua is on the path to transformation into a militaristic and totalitarian state"; "They are trying to transform the revolution into a false God that does not tolerate criticism."[72]

Upon his return, Mons. Obando refused to enter into dialogue with the priests in government or with other ecclesiastic groups. On July 3, the bourgeoisie organized in Masaya a celebration in honor of Obando, during which numerous charismatic groups organized and proclaimed Obando a "prophet" of the Nicaraguan people. A few weeks later, La Prensa led a campaign to honor Obando, and the Venezuelan government awarded him the Order of Francisco Miranda (who was a Mason!). Clearly, with these facts, we see the irreversible conversion of Obando into the indisputable leader of the middle class opposition -- a process which occurred at the same time as the propaganda offensive was unleashed in August by several Protestant groups.

Along with this campaign, there was an obvious expansion of religious sects and denominations that had been formed surreptitiously since the victory of the revolution. Currently there are over 100 sects in Nicaragua; 89 are registered, and 20 of them clearly appeared since July 19, 1979. Decals, wall paintings, and loudspeakers began to bombard the Nicaraguan people with phrases such as "Only Christ saves," "Prepare yourself, Christ is coming," "The end of the world is coming," "Only Jesus liberates," "One must be militant for peace and against hatred," "Repent, Christ is the only way." Groups of specially trained young people went from house to house in the urban districts and in the rural areas carrying pamphlets and asking help for their religious campaigns. Uncharacteristically, in a nation of scarce resources, modern equipment and methods of commercial advertising were used both in printed matter and during meetings. Sects sponsored concerts, dances, and festivals in popular places where professional agitators carefully mixed religious matters with political jokes and music. Large quantities of religious pamphlets came into the nation, produced by outside people, printed by companies with branches in Mexico, Uruguay, and Guatemala. Some well-known lecturers were brought into the country. Among others, Morris Cerrulo was prohibited entry because prior to his arrival he had declared that he was coming to help in "the great and urgent task of undoing the satanical work that is prevalent in that nation." The most notorious campaigns were "Nicaragua for Christ," "Nicaragua 1981," "Interdenominational Area," and "The Harvest of the 1000 Days."

The most notorious religious sect was the Jehovah's Witnesses, which did not accept laws, governmental authority, patriotic symbols, political acts, or the use of arms. In their bulletins they stated, for example, that "Upon denying the mixture of religion and politics, you are following the example of Christ. You can show your faith in the Kingdom of God, the only solution to our many problems, which the politicians are not able to resolve" (Despertad, Aug. 6, 1981).

Furthermore, Jehovah's Witnesses maintained that "In order to eliminate poverty, sickness, corruption and all other ills, God is the answer, the only one who can achieve this." In this manner, they encouraged fatalism, as well as nonparticipation in the health campaigns, in the process of economic recovery, and in the mass organizations. Also, they preached submission to the landowners and anti-unionism: "In general, the bosses have enough problems with personnel, don't contribute to these problems, be a fountain of peace and not one of discussion. Don't view your employer as intrinsically an exploiter. It is most probable that work well done will be compensated" (Atalaya, no. 15). In like manner, they encouraged the rejection of military service and insisted that Jesus said "All those who take up the sword will perish by the sword" and that a fundamental commandment is "Thou shall not kill."

Other Protestant sects included the United States-based Mormons. Having an obvious anticommunist bent, which identified Sandinismo with communism, this group prohibited their followers from any participation in the mass organizations. Seventh Day Adventists, who also opposed the use of arms and worshiped on Saturdays, held an idealized vision of history involving "the struggle between virtue and vice, good and evil, truth and error."[73] They inculcated fatalism and blind obedience: "What should I do to be saved? Believe, repent and obey."[74] Similarly, some Moravians, although not members of their hierarchy, became involved in activities of direct military propaganda, and logistical support for bands of Somocistas who operated in the Zelaya zone with the Misquito population. This was the case in "Operation Red Christmas" at the end of 1981. Thus, the old anticommunist fears introduced by North American missions and spread by the followers of Somoza were utilized.[75]

---

* Despertad and Atalaya, publications of Jehovah's Witnesses, are designed for mass circulation.

In the meantime, the Catholic conflict concerning the priests in government was temporarily resolved when the hierarchy allowed these men to continue in their posts as long as they abstained from participation in any religious activities until they left their posts. This resolution occurred in July 1981. A little while later, however, the hierarchy closed the seminary at Managua, because the hierarchy did not like the direction the seminary was taking, since Mexican teachers were trying to produce Nicaraguan clergy that would address the social needs of the country (September, 1981).

In the following months, Mons. Obando entered La Prensa's "Pro-Liberty Commission" composed of the middle-class parties to advocate freedom of the opposition to destabilize the revolutionary process, creating an internal climate favorable to foreign intervention. On the occasion of his birthday, Mons. Obando received pompous homage from the middle class; and La Prensa published a special edition, dedicated to him, which included 46 photographs. The Venezuelan government awarded Obando the Order of Simon Bolivar, while calling Obando "the prophet and defender of Nicaraguan liberties."

The cult of personality surrounding Obando has been effectively utilized by the middle class, complete with decorations, silver platters, homage, flattering references which describe Obando as "our pastor, the one who guides us, teaches us, and allows us to endure. The price of fidelity to God has always been the enmity of many men. We are with you, cost what it may."[76] Obando has presented himself as being magnanimous to the Sandinista leaders, such as when he asked that there be prayers for the authorities. "This concept of praying for the authorities is still valid even though the authority is exercised by an impious person or an Atheist."[77] In this way, the middle class used anticommunist fears, as spread by imperialism for so many years, and tried to equate Sandinismo with atheistic communism. They claimed that the FSLN was subtly trying to implant atheistic communism through texts, scholarships to socialist countries, propaganda, and a master plan of infiltration in the churches by agents disguised as preachers and priests.

Furthermore, the middle class, with the advice of experts in the techniques of propaganda, have known how to utilize the newspaper La Prensa, their radio stations, and other media, such as gossip and humor and posters and slogans, to generate a climate of fear and tension. Several studies on the utilization of those sophisticated techniques have shown similarities to the documented campaigns which were previously utilized in Chile to prepare for the fall of Allende and in Jamaica to thwart the re-election of Manley.[78]

We have observed the use of words such as <u>love</u>, <u>peace</u>, <u>God</u>, and <u>violence</u>, which possess affective qualities for the Nicaraguan people. For example, there was the juxtaposition in the middle-class newspaper of a photo of young Christians singing and another in which Sandinistas appeared symbolized by the concepts of "hate, violence, and Marxism."[79] Similarly, another case was analyzed, in which through contextual association of headlines the Sandinistas were pictured as false prophets denounced in the gospels.[80]

By the end of 1981, the contra infiltration from Honduras had become serious. "Operation Red Christmas," a plan to commit acts of sabotage against the economy, was revealed. This, together with the flight of Misquito Indians deceived by some Moravian pastors and pro-imperialist leaders, such as Steadman Fagoth, demonstrated the necessity of relocating the Misquito people who inhabited the borders of the Río Coco in order to guarantee their safety and defend the frontier. Simultaneously, the directors of COSEP published a provocative communiqué in violation of the Law of Emergency. They and the leaders of the Communist Party, who encouraged strikes and boycotts against the economy, were tried under the provisions of that law.

In January 1982, when the Central American Democratic Community (the Forum for Peace and Democracy, as it was called by the Reagan administration) was formed for the purpose of isolating Nicaragua, Mons. Obando travelled to the United States, invited by the Institute for Religion and Democracy, an organization intimately connected to the Reagan administration and which has been accused of having CIA connections. Mons. Obando succeeded in obtaining, as was later proved, a donation of $40,000 to discredit the Nicaraguan revolution. In the words of a North American journalist, "The Nicaraguan archbishop appeared to be a political messenger from [Nicaraguan] private enterprise, <u>La Prensa</u> and the opposition parties because he repeated arguments used very often by these parties against the revolution: Cuban advisors, Marxist tendencies, atheistic leaders, a large army, the closings of <u>La Prensa</u>, the imprisonment of the leaders of COSEP, and the loss of public confidence."[81]

Simultaneously, the anti-Marxist preaching by religious factions continued. The outstanding occurrence at this time was the "exposé" of Ministry of Education (MEP) documents in which religious factions critically tried to expose the materialistic theory of knowledge, which they attributed to the Sandinistas. The forces of the Center for Religious Studies joined Mons. Vega who said, "[Groups of] this orientation are saying that there is an intense and organized materialistic indoctrination [which] is a direct mockery of Christianity . . . because work is more than a simple materialistic show of energy since work needs creative ideas, and inventive mental faculties." In the meantime, La Prensa took advantage of the antisocialistic position of the Vatican by printing the following statement below a photo of the Pope: "John Paul II knows Marxism and its practices better than any other priest. He lived in Poland under a communist government for more than thirty years. Now he is fighting to eradicate it from the church and in particular, from the order of the Jesuits."[82] Thus the middle class took the opportunity to spread the fear that communism would infiltrate the church itself and to attack the Jesuits, an order which had distinguished itself by opting to help the poor of Central America.

It was at this juncture, the beginning of 1982, that the Episcopal Conference (CEN) issued its slanderous declaration about the relocation of some of the Misquito population away from the Honduran border. The Episcopal Conference reiterated the falsehoods stated by the North American government. Among other things, this declaration classified as mere political "adversaries" the bands that had assassinated nearly one hundred farmers, women, and children in the previous months. It compared the supposed Sandinista repression of the Misquitos to the repression of the Salvadoran and Guatemalan people, and utilized language that depicted a climate of terror and tragedy in that region. Unquestionably, the Episcopal Conference held the revolutionary government totally responsible. These charges were made even though it was known that the Reagan administration had approved 19 million dollars for CIA-backed contra activities to destabilize the revolutionary government and was frantically looking for proof to show to Congress and the rest of the world in order to justify its intervention in Central America. The Nicaraguan government, in this same period, was consolidating its national unity through the discussion of the law of political parties, the release of the COSEP leaders, and the announcement of a plan of incentives for private producers. The Permanent Conference of Political Parties of Latin America (COPPPAL) was also meeting in Nicaragua at this time. Thus these religious organizations simultaneously prohibited their personnel from taking part in the tasks of the revolution on the grounds that priests and religious figures should not take part in politics, and they used their influence on believers to foster a pro-imperialist policy.

The next conflict occurred during Holy Week when, because of the imminent threat of intervention, the Government of National Reconstruction decided to suspend vacations. This was publicized by the middle class as "another example of religious persecution in Nicaragua," while the Episcopal Conference opposed working on those days "traditionally reserved for religion." Nevertheless, the government authorized workers to leave work to attend religious ceremonies on Holy Thursday or Friday. At the same time, they pointed out that it was the first time that the middle classes, which were accustomed to spending this week of sloth at the beaches or at drunken parties, had ever been so fervently concerned with liturgical acts.

A little later, on the first of May, while the working class stated that "we defend the revolution for the construction of socialism," the middle class, through their spokesperson, Mons. Obando, demanded the freedom and independence of unions. In a public meeting of the opposition political parties of the Coordinadora Democrática, the archbishop said that "the unions must keep their independence vis-à-vis everyone: the private owner, the public owner and the state which tends to make of them a transmission belt."[83]

The middle class again took up the cry for peace in Central America by calling for peace in Nicaragua, which, for them, was threatened by class hatred, which they identified with "class violence" [turbas]." Again the hierarchy echoed this message and proclaimed it in several sermons and religious acts: "We beg God to make Nicaragua over so that we may live in true peace."[84] The hierarchy's interpretation of the class struggle was to consider it a subjective and voluntary phenomenon. The middle class attempted to identify it with the word "hatred" in order to remove any sense of Christian validity from the concept and to deny its objective existence in reality. Thus, Mons. Obando said that

"Hatred can be engendered with relative ease if one suffers jealousy, envy, resentment, or negative thinking. Therefore, political agitators take advantage of this fact to foment envy and discontent among their followers and thus, lead them to extreme hatred against another social class or against another country."[85]

This criticism of violence was directed against the formation of popular militias and against the consolidation of the army, especially to prevent the participation of Christians in the army to defend the nation in case of aggression. Conciliation among classes, nonviolent methods of change, and pardon granted toward oppressors are the proper "Christian" concepts for the middle classes. In the eyes of the middle class, Christ's preference for the poor refers to the poor in spirit, not to a social class. Thus, the Episcopal Conference included under the concept of poor, the elderly, the imprisoned, the suffering, and the lonely, as well as widows and the unemployed.[86]

The ideological maneuver that the bourgeoisie carried out was to invert reality in order to hide its responsibility for the class struggle which was brought about by its unjust appropriation of the means of production. Thus, they referred to the literacy crusade as "domestication," to the revolutionary state as "a corrupt and bad administration," to the FSLN as a new "armed oligarchy," and to the relations with socialist countries as "dependence on Russian imperialism." In the same manner, the middle class and its religious spokesmen, "instead of seeing themselves as the exploiter, affirm[ed] instead that their class [was] the legitimate possessor of fundamental values such as God, order, liberty, justice and love. Thus, under this guise of religion, the bourgeoisie [had] obscured its role as the group which [was] really responsible for the class struggle."[87]

More recently (August 1982), the religious crisis exploded with unusual violence because of a series of events. In the barrio of Santa Rosa, a popular priest, Arias Caldera, was abruptly transferred by Archbishop Obando. A protest against this transfer led to an unfortunate physical incident with Mons. Bosco Vivas, when he tried to remove the chalice in the chapel of Santa Rosa. A skirmish occurred, and as a result many parishioners were excommunicated. The publicizing of an amorous affair of one of the spokesmen of the Archbishopric, Father Bismarck Carballo, also worsened relations, as did the seizure of Protestant churches throughout the country, and the hostility shown toward Mons. Obando on August 14 while he was celebrating mass in Masaya. Confrontations within several Catholic high schools also occurred, as well as an armed attack against a popular demonstration perpetrated at a Salesian high school in Masaya, which resulted in one death and several injuries (among pro-government demonstrators). The school was temporarily taken over by the Ministry of Popular Education, and the Episcopal Conference issued a statement opposing that intervention. We must add all this to the distortion of the news carried out by in-ternational news agencies, to the invectives against the government published in the Sunday newssheet of the Archdiocese of Managua, to the crippling blows of the Catholic radio station, and to the calumny originated in a newspaper declaration given by Obando that the government had detained the bishop of the Atlantic Coast.[88]

Clearly, the middle class and the imperialists achieved their objectives at this juncture: to force the government into open confrontation, which would go beyond the limits of fair debate, through provocation for the purpose of showing "the authentic struggle between the exploiter and the exploited, which was presented as the religious struggle between God and the devil, Christianity and atheism, the institutional church and the FSLN; the definite struggle of our people against the revolution."[89] This political/ religious crisis was rich in lessons for Nicaraguans. It demonstrated that religious institutions can be used as a privileged domain by the bourgeoisie and that these institutions, which have demonstrated their skill in portraying government acts as religious persecution, could have tremendous national and international impact in defaming the Sandinista revolution. Fortunately, errors committed by revolutionary sectors in the handling of the crisis were subsequently the object of very healthy self-criticism which resulted in the termination of popular occupation of Protestant church buildings and a renewed effort at dialogue.

The Communiqué of the Episcopal Conference on August 24, 1982, rehashed old slanderous arguments concerning the harassment of religious sectors, the right of the family to educate their children in Christian fashion, the right of the church to own educational centers, and the need to counterattack materialist ideologies. But the bishops also said, "We exhort the faithful to struggle for the Christian education of their children." This was a clear call to confrontation -- be it ideological, economic, or military -- with the government. In other words, religious institutions had slowly been converted into a key ideological instrument of the bourgeoisie and of imperialism. This process arrived at its most extreme expression in the sanctifying of the systematic contra attacks from Honduras which have cost more than 300 lives and untold damage. The culmination of the process of identification which we have been exploring was also expressed in the slogans which the ex-National Guardsmen and mercenary contras used when they periodically attacked Nicaragua's people and Nicaragua's borders: "Long live God and death to Sandino-communism" and "Long live religion, death to atheism."

In conclusion, we believe we have proved our initial hypothesis that religious institutions have been converted into a fundamental channel for the reproduction of the dominant ideology of the Somoza years. But one might ask whether the participation of revolutionary Christians in religious institutions made a lie of this hypothesis. We believe that it did not, based on two fundamental considerations that need an empirical investigation to support them but are relatively obvious. First, we have already noted that religious institutions do not by definition include all those who are baptized or those who sporadically participate in church matters but, rather, religious institutions such as the Catholic Church are more accurately represented by their professional or permanent core of workers. We view these institutions, especially the Catholic Church, as having a structure of vertical and hierarchical power, in which the concentration of strength favors the middle sectors since they occupy positions of power. In other words, dedicated rank and file Christians have a minimum of influence when they belong to the Catholic Church. Also, they find themselves bound by principles of fidelity, obedience, discipline, and unity to the decisions of their hierarchical leaders who ally themselves with the bourgeoisie.

The second reason which allows us to support our hypothesis is the following: since July 19, 1979, with the exception of several farming areas, Nicaragua has not observed any growth in the institutional revolutionary Christian sector -- quite the contrary. The abandonment of the church can be explained by several reasons. For some, the contradiction between membership in an institution led by people of the middle classes and their commitment to liberation is unacceptable. For others, the practice of Christianity does not necessitate a traditional church institution; one can express Christian practice in health or education campaigns or in tasks which show one's love of mankind. According to the Gospel, "Through your works shall ye be known." Finally, others have opted to give their full time to revolutionary organizations, renouncing their past beliefs in favor of giving their fidelity to some versions of Marxism which condemn all religious expression as "the tool of bourgeois idealists." (We will return to this later).

AN ANALYSIS OF RELIGIOUS PHENOMENA AND THEIR POLITICAL IMPLICATIONS

In this section we shall try to respond briefly to the question: How did religious institutions become the privileged ideological transmitters of the bourgeoisie? And also we will discuss the political consequences which correspond to the analysis of religion which was set forth in the previous section.

Political Manipulation

The first and easiest explanation attributes religious problems to political manipulation by the forces of imperialism and the bourgeoisie. The evidence is overwhelming with respect to North American policy which was revamped in the Rockefeller Report (1969) and implemented by the CIA by means of infiltration, abductions, assassination, and manipulation of religious organizations especially in the decade of the 1970's[90]. More recently, the Report of Santa Fe has outlined the policies of the Reagan administration and stated:

> The foreign policy of the United States must begin to confront, and not simply to react ex post facto, to the theology of liberation as it is utilized in Latin America by the clergy of "liberation theology" . . . . The role of the church in Latin America is vital for the concept of political liberty. Lamentably, Marxist forces have utilized the church as a political weapon against private property and the capitalist system of production, infiltrating the religious community with ideas which are less Christian than communist.[91]

That is to say, for the Reagan administration the function of the church was to defend the capitalist system. Those opposed to this idea were "communist infiltrators." These are precisely the same arguments that we heard from the Nicaraguan bourgeoisie and their religious spokespersons. The methods used to carry out these manipulations have been financial help (for example the 5 million dollar donation offered by the American government in 1982, destined for COSEP and the Catholic hierarchy, which was refused by the Nicaraguan government), the distortion of religious issues through U.S. channels of communication, support for the activities of CELAM and numerous sects and denominations, invitations for speaking tours, endowments, and homage.

For imperialism, Christian participation in the revolutionary process is a dangerous example -- we can see the consequences in El Salvador and Guatemala -- for all of Christian and exploited Latin America. The prediction of Ché Guevara echoes ominously: "The day on which Christians take seriously their commitment to the liberation of the poor, on this day, Latin America will take a great leap toward its liberty."

Similarly, we have seen how the Nicaraguan bourgeoisie have cleverly cultivated their personal ties with the Catholic hierarchy and other Protestant personalities, because they know very well the impact upon the popular mind of these religious figures. Besides, Christian practices constitute the perfect disguise with which to hide economic and political interests.

Undoubtedly, the explanation of direct and indirect political manipulation is valid, although it should not be considered the only causal factor, as it frequently is. Because if we see the clergy as propagandists in the service of imperialism, and religious practices as a simple means of alienating the people in favor of the counterrevolution, then we must resort also to a direct political response. In other words, this view would lead to a direct confrontation which implies the closing of churches, the chastisement of religious workers, the denunciation of all preaching as a product of the Yankees, and the categorization of all believers as counter-revolutionaries. A unilateral categorization of religious phenomena as political manipulation, pure and simple, neglects the specific character of all ideology (its characteristics, origins, laws, and changes) and brings one to the use of political or military methods to combat an ideological phenomenon, risking the conversion of an anti-imperialist fight into an anti-religious crusade. This is precisely what the counter-revolution seeks -- that is to say, the polarization of "believers" on one side, and the "atheist" revolutionary sector on the other side, simultaneously presenting the Popular Sandinista Revolution as opposed to freedom of belief and expression, with the goal of isolating the revolution.

Political methods can apparently crush an ideological offensive, but they cannot overcome it dialectically. The contradiction survives in a latent manner as in the calm which followed the above-mentioned "storms" of August and September 1982.

Bourgeois Ideology and Christianity

Although Christianity was born as the expression of the exploited sectors of the Roman Empire, it was converted, after Emperor Constantine's co-optation of the Catholic hierarchy in 315, and after more than 1700 years of being utilized by the exploiting classes (slave masters, feudal lords, and finally, capitalists), into a religion laden with practices, norms, beliefs, and ideological justifications of oppression.

Almost from the beginning, Christianity was burdened with an enormous ideological weight. It became, sometimes innocently, a carrier of ideology. We must realize that it is precisely this "innocence" which gives an ideology of domination its essential characteristics. An ideology of domination destroys man's capacity to understand the subjective nature of values and knowledge and their political ties which defend a specific social class. Therefore, we must recognize that the bourgeois ideological substance which has such a hold on Christianity in Nicaragua today is not the simple product of the bourgeoisie and of imperialism, but rather the result of the centuries-old process of the assimilation of concepts and values of a system called "Christianity," characterized by the intervention of political power on behalf of the church so that it might achieve its pastoral work (Pablo Richard). In the final analysis, the manipulation exists precisely because it has been very easy for the bourgeoisie, with their accumulated experience (let us recognize the Christian teachings of the feudal and slave classes, when, for example, the Kingdom of God was converted into a future goal or dream and not a concrete task of the present), to maintain exploitation in feudal, slave, and capitalist systems.

The emphasis which is given by the most reactionary religious sectors to the "primacy of the spiritual" as the "highest and most fundamental aspect of life and of history . . . the level where man becomes a person" synthesizes bourgeois idealism by means of a fleshless and metaphysical theology. The "spiritual" is presented in their discussions as if it were a level which is autonomous from the world and from politics, an environment without conflict where peace reigns. It is there that the work of the church is supposedly located. This is why these clergy consider themselves the most appropriate agents to mediate political conflicts--since they are above partisanship. In addition, since they consider liberation as the eradication of individual sin, they see the political formulation of liberation as an attempt to substitute the function of religion and to confuse the spiritual and temporal levels, bringing conflict into the midst of ecclesiastical unity.

The thesis of the unity and conciliation of classes is a bourgeois reformist project of the "Democratic-Christian" or "Social-Democratic" type, whose religious expression is the "overcoming of hatred," "pardon for one who offends you," and "brotherhood among sons of the same father." This discussion, that we are not going to explore in great depth here, contains much internal coherence, and of course, complementarity with the global ideological discourse of the bourgeoisie, which in many cases is the only religious discourse the bourgeoisie have known since infancy -- an opaque veil which prevents them from understanding the objective function of their ideology, which is to hide class struggle and imperialist economic exploitation.

What political implications does this have? Simply, the understanding that ideological change is not an issue that could be quickly resolved nor a question of methods which can take advantage of emotional slogans or of verbal discussions. What is called for is a conscientizing methodology, theory, and practice, which occurs simultaneously with changes in economics and politics and law. But relations between bourgeois ideology and Christianity do not end here.

One must realize that, fortunately, never in history have the dominant ideologies succeeded in completely "brainwashing" the oppressed classes. If they had, there never would have been class struggle as "the motor of history" in military, economic, political, and ideological conflicts. And Christianity has not remained apart from these conflicts in its messages and practices, which, given the symbolic nature of religious discussion, has permitted it much ambiguity,⁹² in accordance with social class.

Historically, the popular classes have succeeded in maintaining a religious interpretation and some religious practices which have expressed their interests through "the protest against real poverty"; and, further, in periods of revolutionary fervor, as in Nicaragua in the 1970's, Christian faith served as an inducement to fight against the dictatorship. Cases abound, from the most famous such as that of the Solentiname community or the youth of the Revolutionary Christian Movement, to the most anonymous ones of so many peasants who, for love of their neighbor and in defense of the God of life, collaborated in the Sandinista fight. Fr. Gaspar García Laviana said: "My faith and my membership in the Catholic church compelled me to take an active part in the revolutionary process with the FSLN, because the liberation of an oppressed people was an integral part of the total redemption of Christ." This motivation by faith did not exclude a scientific Marxist analysis of reality, nor the use of its methods for the taking of power and the implementation of social change. This reality has been recognized by the National Directorate of the FSLN in their Communiqué Concerning Religion, but is unknown to those who interpret religious phenomena on the basis of theoretical reflections from other contexts and epochs.

The vulgar Marxist vision, based on the judgment of authorities more than on historical verification, can be summarized in a phrase which was extrapolated from a very profound text of Marx: "Religion is the opiate of the people." This statement has been used to present opposition to a revolutionary ideology which critics claimed would be materialist, scientific, and atheist, as opposed to a bourgeois ideology which would be idealist, anti-scientific, and religious. This position tried, ahistorically, to absolutize the analysis of religion. But, Carlos Fonseca, who recognized the danger of absolutizing religion, cautioned:

> We must be careful that theories of progress are part of our concrete practice, because if they are not we will fall into a sterile dogmatism . . . . In this regard what can help us a great deal is the very modest theoretical tradition of our organization. In the F.S.L.N. theory has been related to the practical development of our movement . . . . One must understand Nicaragua's national reality with the eyes of a Marxist theorist and to read Marxist theory with Nicaraguan eyes.

This interpretation of the religious problem in today's Nicaragua would be irrelevant if it did not have clear political implications. For instance, it relates to the examination of the question of whether or not it is possible for a believer to participate in revolutionary organizations. Is it necessary to treat the believer with suspicion, seeing him as an opportunist who tries to save his church from the revolutionary crisis by putting on the Sandinista uniform? This vision corresponds to the position that considers Christian participation in the revolutionary process a tactical alliance which has to be adopted for the good of the revolution at this point but which later on can be excluded. In other words, this position ignores the principle of mutual respect and autonomy of the political and religious realms which the Communiqué of the FSLN affirms. It also ignores the fact that in the ranks of the FSLN there is room for believers who through their behavior have demonstrated a total commitment to the cause of the people.

The hypothesis of incompatibility between Marxism and Christianity is, paradoxically, the position of the bourgeoisie and of dogmatic factions of the Revolution -- even though their subjective intentions might be different, the results are objectively the same.*

However, the position of our National Directorate permits a differentiation between religious sectors according to their praxis. Thus the revolution is strengthened by believers committed to the liberation of the people. Besides, this position may help arrest the abandonment of participation in church matters by revolutionary believers because of the confusion that the supposed contradiction between being Marxist and Christian -- propagated by various manuals in current use -- generates in them. To the extent that this abandonment has taken place, it has allowed the bourgeoisie to dominate religious institutions and acts and has significantly debilitated the revolutionary camp and its capacity to respond ideologically to the bourgeoisie in this "game" that they have been playing. When we see the nefarious consequences of this false dichotomy -- which are just as palpable as the positive participation of believers in the revolutionary process -- we cannot keep from asking "Who is the idealist here and now?"

The Internal Structure of Religious Institutions

Another explanatory factor in understanding how the churches and religious sects are critical to the perpetuation of bourgeois ideology in the revolutionary process is to be found in the internal structure of these institutions. Here we refer particularly to churches like the Catholic Church, an institution with a legal system (canon law) which is hundreds of years old and is based on norms which originated in feudal Europe when the church was the greatest authority on the European continent. The church was organized as a

---

* I do not deny the validity of such an incompatibility between a certain version of Marxism (which emphasizes materialism or economic determinism) and a certain version of Christianity (which is idealist, liberal, or pietistic). Unfortunately, these versions are perhaps the most common.

pyramid of power with an authoritarian style of behavior. As a general rule, the participation of the faithful in the discussion and formation of decisions is minimal. Of course, there exist great variations in some Protestant denominations, which are much more decentralized and democratic. And the Catholic Church, too, has experienced changes as a result of Vatican II and the Latin American Bishops Conferences, especially that of Medellín (1968).

Nevertheless, the training of a large part of the clergy, especially those found in positions of authority and those now of advanced age, evolved from a theological education which preceded the concepts which developed in the decade of the 1960's and can be summarized as liberation theology. A religious education which was metaphysical, encyclopedic, theoretical, and routinized, which encouraged personal relations of discipline and submission to authority and rules, has resulted in the formation of a certain type of religious mentality which is thoroughly permeated with adherence to bourgeois ideology. This education led a segment of the clergy to convert itself into an ally of the middle classes once these clergymen found themselves in positions of leadership outside the seminary.

Furthermore, one must consider that these institutions are not limited to the national scene, but form part of a worldwide structure which possesses a specific global policy and transcends local concerns. For example, many of the Protestant denominations and churches are subordinate to their central offices in the United States, where the leadership generally supports the principles of North American capitalism. It is with great difficulty that these individuals reject the ideological positions which predominate in their parishes because the North American people have been anesthetized, in large measure, by the formidable ideology of the most powerful bourgeoisie in the world.

In the case of the Catholic Church, the "third way" position of the Vatican was well known: that is to say, the thesis of the coexistence of the bourgeoisie and the proletariat with the exploitation of the latter attenuated by the concept of "social well-being" and some worker participation in industry. But, especially in light of a recent financial scandal in which a high church official was involved, Vatican involvement with a variety of multinational corporations must be acknowledged.

Clearly the fundamental interest of religious institutions lies in maintaining and amplifying their power, political as well as economic and ideological, even though for them that which is political and economic might be "means" towards a pastoral "end." This "ecclesiocentrism" is seen in the institutions' position toward anything which questions or weakens their own power. This is their central political norm -- of even greater weight than ideological principles.

Historically, we have in Nicaragua the example of the Catholic hierarchy in the time of José Santos Zelaya (1893-1909), when it opposed "liberalism," accusing it of atheism and persecuting the people's religious faith simply because the Liberal government had confiscated its lands, cemeteries, administrative records, and schools. The hierarchy then joined forces with the conservatives and with Yankee imperialism to destroy the Liberal government. Nevertheless, after the fall of Zelaya, after the massive penetration of North American capital, accompanied by Protestant churches, this same hierarchy publicly denounced the "imperialist penetration which trampled on our honour and sovereignty." The real interest of the Catholic hierarchy was not in opposing imperialism but rather in blocking anyone who made attempts on their power, temporal or spiritual, be they Liberals, Protestants, or Sandinistas. Today the Sandinista government does not attempt to curtail the spiritual power of the Church, but rather its temporal privileges of a previous time such as the right to unilaterally control instruction in Catholic secondary schools, to utilize the means of communication according to its fanciful wishes, to receive financial donations from the U.S.

In addition, the religious hierarchy sees itself as a competitor with the Sandinistas for the mobilization and allegiance of the masses. It laments the fact that "now the people do not consult us, worship us or serve us as they did before"; that is to say, their influence upon the masses has decreased with advances in education, health, the growth of the mass organizations, and all the achievements of the revolution.

This interpretation of religious-political phenomena in Nicaragua is without doubt valid, but as in the previous cases, it is valid provided that one does not overgeneralize it. To do so would be to conclude that religious institutions are simply affiliates of a pro-imperialist international power, and that it is impossible to expect any positive change in them except a simple tactical accommodation in order to survive in a future socialist system with some measure of power, although less than that which they enjoyed under capitalism. This vision must be amplified with previous explanations and with references to our reality where we see the possibility of much flexibility within ecclesiastical institutions, with much autonomy, decision-making, and religious practice. We must also take into consideration the situation in other countries, such as in Brazil, where important sectors of religious institutions are in the vanguard of the fight for liberation of that suffering people, and in Cuba, where religious institutions have changed to work effectively within a revolutionary context. This last consideration permits Nicaraguans to develop a more flexible and accurate political practice with respect to religion in their nation.

Religion and the Means of Production

Religion is an aspect of reality situated in a social context with specific structures (family, ethnic, productive, etc.) of which the most important is the socioeconomic or the mode of production. Productive relationships and forces determine the limits and tendencies of religious phenomena. The impact of the mode of production on ideological matters is not synonymous with mechanical or unidirectional causality; rather, it constitutes "that which determines, in the long run, social consciousness."

In Nicaragua the reproduction of ideology is not simply the product of the ideological influences of institutions like the church. It corresponds fundamentally to the perpetuation of the capitalist relationships of production which can be found in the framework of the mixed economy and the economic planning appropriate for the private sector. Whether for geopolitical reasons or because of the underdevelopment of the productive forces (including human and administrative resources), the reproduction of capitalist relations also signifies, on the political level, pluralism and participation in the management of the state, and on the ideological level, it implies the existence of La Prensa and other opposition channels.

In addition, the underdevelopment of the productive forces means, for example, the existence of a peasant sector almost at the mercy of natural forces, given the lack of irrigation and agricultural technology. If one gives credence to counterrevolutionary rumors, the agricultural conditions and natural disasters such as the recent flooding or droughts can be attributed to divine punishment of the "atheistic Sandinista" government or a sign that Nicaraguans must give reverence to a religious figure so that divine favor will assure them a good harvest. In this case, one can see how religious beliefs and the mode of production are united in the concept of ideology.

This explanation of religion in Nicaragua permits us to understand politically that the transformation of the bourgeois ideology which impregnated Christianity is not something that could be achieved in the short run; nor could it be resolved only at the ideological level. The problem is of a structural nature; the formation of the new man will not be the quick result of good intentions, information campaigns, or laws, but will occur with the dialectical change in the superstructure <u>and</u> the infrastructure.

In opposition to those who feel that the role of Marxists ought to be that of advocating intransigent atheistic propaganda, the Cuban Communist Party recently recognized that, according to Marx, "the task of Communists does not entail the conversion of all to atheism, but rather the revolutionary transformation in the world through the destruction of all relations in which man is humble, subjugated, defenseless and degraded" (Thesis and Resolutions, of the First Congress of the Cuban Communist Party).

This vision of structural transformation does not mean that we must abandon religious ideological struggles. One must remember that there exists a dialectic relationship between ideology and social change and that the realm of religion possesses a "seeming autonomy" based on the following factors: 1) religion produces "goods" such as publications, buildings, rites, lectures and courses; 2) religion develops an institutional dimension with specific objectives such as the conservation and amplification of its power to produce religious "goods," extend its following, and avoid internal decomposition; 3) there exist specific conflicts in the religious realm such as those between the hierarchy and the lower clergy for institutional control, between the clergy and the laity, and between institutional rigidity and the personal charisma of each religious individual.[93]

The recognition of this relative autonomy implies politically that, in order to understand the complexity of religion, we must consider the characteristics, contradictions, and specific dynamics of a given religion. For example, one sociological hypothesis of religious dynamics affirms that "a religion ought to maintain its historical continuity and its tradition and respect the limits of its origins and organization; it must also conserve its power and satisfy the demands of its officials and its public, while rationally utilizing its resources."

If we apply this hypothesis to the Nicaraguan case, we understand the propensity of all religion to historical continuity, as an intrinsic necessity of religion. We cannot expect a complete change of traditional Christian practices, which are permeated with bourgeois ideology. As in the case of popular culture, what we hope for is a recovery of its most valuable characteristics and a discarding of its most harmful ones. That has been the attitude of the Nicaraguan government with regard to popular fiestas such as that of Santo Domingo, during which there has been an attempt to control alcoholism, prostitution, and violence, so that the specifically religious content of popular festivity can be developed. In like manner, what has been removed from the Christmas celebration has been its utilization for mercantile purposes by the bourgeoisie. The process is gradual and its primary responsibility does not belong to the Nicaraguan government nor to the FSLN, but to Christians committed through their political convictions and their faith to the "preferential option for the poor."

The Dynamics of the Revolutionary Process

Here we will briefly analyze some aspects of the complicated dialectic now taking place in the Sandinista revolutionary process which may help in the understanding of religious problems.

In the first place, the insurrection succeeded relatively rapidly in the taking of military and political power in part because the Somoza dictatorship did not permit minimal liberties to the middle class. This hastened the disintegration of the dominant ideology and permitted the foundation of a "hegemony" in the Gramscian sense, built upon the popular sectors. Yet, at the same time, rapid revolutionary advances in the political-military field were out of phase with relative backwardness in the ideological and economic fields. Also, the fact that religious institutions had served as places for the expression of opposition to the dictatorship and as organizing channels for the revolutionary forces gave these institutions--like La Prensa--a legitimacy in the eyes of the public and the international community, which today is advantageous to the bourgeoisie in its clever use of them.

The fact that military-political advances have been out of phase with those in the ideological realm has meant that we have tended to over-politicize what we consider "ideological" and to interpret what we considered to be "religious" exclusively from a political perspective. Thus, we have utilized political methods to fight ideological battles in the field of religion. This problem of lack of phase has also been reflected in the fact that the leaders of the revolution have exhibited greater capacity in things

99

political and military (it had to be this way in order to defeat the dictatorship) than in ideological matters. And this adds to the complexity of the ideological issue.

In the second place, the constant imperialist aggression, which began with Reagan's assumption of power, has clearly conditioned the dynamics of the revolutionary process. The economic, ideological, military, and political power of the United States has fallen with disproportionate weight upon Nicaragua and has affected all aspects of life, directly or indirectly. The climate of increasing tensions has compelled the Nicaraguan government to declare the state of emergency, to restrict freedom of expression by the middle-class opposition, and to delay the government's plans for economic recovery. Thus the middle classes, upon finding restrictions on the channels of expression on which they previously relied, have been compelled to turn to the only institution which was autonomous from the revolutionary state: the churches and religious sects. The middle class thus has the advantages that these institutions possess -- national scope, solid organizational structure, ideological messages saturated with middle-class convictions, and personal and political ties of long standing.

On the other hand, the restrictions of the state of emergency were interpreted by many reactionary clerics, who mechanically associated the Sandinista experience with that of Cuba and the Soviet Union, as the prelude to a greatly feared "totalitarianism." In addition, the clear liberal and idealist content of mainstream traditional Christianity easily led many clerics to defend unrestricted individual liberty, the right of ownership of the means of production, bourgeois democracy, and the absolute nonintervention of the state into the separate sphere of social life.

In the third place, since the triumph of the revolution we have observed a doubly contradictory process: on the one hand, we saw people gradually moving toward democratization, in the participation of their voice and vote in the decisions which affected them. On the other hand, we observed that in the religious institutions, especially the Catholic Church, there was a gradual hardening of authoritarianism, a demand for submissive obedience, and the use of sanctions without previous dialogue with "subordinates." Evidently, the democratic thrust of the Popular Sandinista Revolution brought to the people and to the clergy the demand for similar participation within religious institutions. This was especially true now because the churches were not outside of society but immersed in its contradictions. For the

100

hierarchies, this constituted more proof of the
dangerous nature of the Popular Sandinista Revolution
and compelled them to reclaim internal unity on the
basis of unconditional obedience and authority. An
urge for institutional self-preservation within a
vertical and pro-bourgeois model of the church can
clearly be observed in the communiqués of the bishops
as well as in the recent letter of the Pope. Pope
John Paul II indicated: "Around the bishops the unity
of the faithful must be tightly woven" and "a popular
church opposed to the Church guided by its legitimate
pastors is a grave deviation" (June 29, 1982).

At the same time that this contradiction between
popular democracy and institutional authoritarianism
was occurring, another divergence was in the making.
On the one hand, we saw the people moving away from a
magical and naive state of consciousness towards a
critical, scientific awareness fostered by the literacy campaign, adult education, the mass media, and the
mass organizations. At the same time, however, we saw
the middle class and its religious allies moving
towards mysticism and irrationality by means of
"charismatic" experiences, a predisposition toward
magical and miraculous acts, an increase in the number
of empty rites and rituals, and a strong tendency
toward metaphysical spiritualism. What did this
contradictory process mean? First, it meant that the
advance of rational awareness took from the middle
class the most "natural" and pseudoscientific ideological forms of legitimation such as the defense of
liberal democracy as the only form of democracy, the
defense of individual liberty as the true and "genuine" liberty, the arguments of neoclassical economics
about the advantages of the capitalist system, and the
bipolar vision of the world. When the middle classes
were not able to demonstrate with genuine arguments
the validity of their theories and concepts, which
were systematically exposed by the newspapers, radios,
and other revolutionary means of communication, they
came to realize that within religious discourse the
possibility of an ideological defeat was more remote.
The middle class realized that it "had to win" in this
arena, considering the impact of bourgeois ideology on
Christianity and its political connections to representatives of religious institutions.

In addition, the tendency toward mysticism and
irrationality can be interpreted as a means of escape
for the middle class when confronted with the revolutionary process which threatens the material bases of
their existence as a class as well as the ideological
underpinnings of their status. Now they are the
"judged," not those who sit in judgment. Their
retreat to mysticism reflects a desperate search for

compensation in the next life and their wish to escape an ineluctable future. This process, which is not unique to the Sandinista Revolution but is happening worldwide, is interesting to watch. The middle class, which had defeated feudalism centuries ago by proclaiming their faith in The Goddess of Reason against a medieval obscurantist religion, have now changed their views. Now that "the justice of power and the power of justice" have been appropriated by the social class which the bourgeoisie exploited, we see the middle class taking refuge in the "irrationality" and "obscurantism" which they condemned in previous centuries. Now they cling to these religious institutions which they once fought, as if they were shipwrecked and in search of salvation. Nevertheless, objectively, there is no earthly salvation for imperialism, nor for its ecclesiastical accomplices, because when the people make up their mind in an organized and aware manner to fight to pursue their liberation to its ultimate consequences, "there is no human or technological force which can stop them" (P. Arauz).

FOREWORD NOTES

[1]Viewed by Thomas Walker on Sandinista television in June, 1984. Howard Frederick at the Ohio University School of Telecommunications has a videotaped copy of that conversation.

[2]Tayacán, "Psychological Operations in Guerrilla Warfare," translated by the Congressional Research Service Language Services, October 15, 1984. The priest, in the secretly videotaped conversation stresses the need for deaths at an upcoming march. The CIA manual also advises guerrilla leaders to see to it that protest marches result in deaths and therefore, in the creation of martyrs.

[3]Philip Taubman, "Managua Cleric Is Said to Train Sandinista Foes," New York Times, August 1, 1984, pp. 1, 4.

[4]"Sandinista Cleric Defends His Stand," New York Times, December 11, 1984, p. 3. We use this citation from the Times to demonstrate the fact that inaccurate reporting was by no means confined to the more predictably irresponsible sectors of the U.S. mass media such as TV network news, the wire services, and high-circulation weekly newsmagazines.

[5]See, for instance, Michael Dodson and T. S. Montgomery, "The Churches in the Nicaraguan Revolution," in Thomas W. Walker, ed., Nicaragua in Revolution (New York: Praeger, 1982), pp. 161-180.

[6]Some of the most thought-provoking research and writing done in this area is by Thomas C. Bruneau, working in Brazil. See his The Political Transformation of the Brazilian Catholic Church (London: Cambridge University Press, 1974) and The Church in Brazil: The Politics of Religion (Austin: The University of Texas Press, 1982).

[1]When reference is made to Catholic Social doctrine I include within this general category the interpretation of the gospels by the magisterium of the Catholic church; the statements (letters, encyclicals) of the popes and synods of bishops; and the philosophical influence of St. Augustine and St. Thomas Acquinas which has remained a part of Catholic doctrine through the papacy of John Paul II.

[2]"The Church in the Present Day Transformation of Latin America in Light of the Council," in Gremillion, Joseph, The Gospel of Peace and Justice (Maryknoll, N.Y.: Orbis, 1976).

[3]"The Church in the Present Day Transformation of Latin America in Light of the Council," Section III, Nos. 19 & 20 in Gremillion, Joseph, The Gospel of Peace and Justice (Maryknoll, N.Y.: Orbis, 1976), p. 453.

[4]"The Church in the Present Day Transformation of Latin America in Light of the Council," Section II, Nos. 3 & 4 in Gremillion, Joseph, The Gospel of Peace and Justice (Maryknoll, N.Y.: Orbis, 1976), p. 447.

[5]See, for example, Lernoux, Penny, Cry of the People (N.Y., N.Y.: Penguin Books, 1982); Hennelly, Alfred, and Langan, John, eds., Human Rights in the Americas: The Struggle for Consensus (Washington, D.C.: Georgetown University Press, 1982); John Paul II Confronts Liberation Theology (Washington, D.C.: Ethics and Public Policy Center, 1982); Eagleson, John and Scharper, Philip, eds., Puebla and Beyond (Maryknoll, N.Y.: Orbis Books, 1979).

[6]This analysis follows that of Part III, "The Awakening," in Lernoux, Cry of the People (N.Y., N.Y.: Penguin Books, 1982).

[7]Thus, for example, Nicaraguan Archbishop Obando y Bravo could argue that, according to Puebla, the church's option for the poor was preferential but not exclusive. Interview, July 10, 1982.

[8]"The Church in the Present Day Transformation of Latin America in Light of the Council," Section II,

No. 16, in Gremillion, Joseph, The Gospel of Peace and Justice (Maryknoll, N.Y.: Orbis, 1976), p. 460.

[9]Final Document (46) in Eagleson, John and Scharper, Philip, eds., Puebla and Beyond (Maryknoll, N.Y.: Orbis Books, 1979), p. 129.

[10]St. Paul's letters to the Galatians 3:28.

[11]"The Church in the Present Day Transformation of Latin America in Light of the Council," Section II, No. 5, in Gremillion, Joseph, The Gospel of Peace and Justice (Maryknoll, N.Y.: Orbis, 1976), p. 447.

[12]Conferencia Episcopal de Nicaragua a los hombres de buena voluntad; August 3, 1978.

[13]Ibid.

[14]Ibid.

[15]An excellent discussion of the Catholic position on human rights is to be found in Hollenbach, David, S.J., "Global Human Rights: An Interpretation of the Contemporary Catholic Understanding" in Hennelly, Alfred and Langan, John, eds., Human Rights in the Americas: The Struggle for Consensus (Washington, D.C.: Georgetown University Press, 1982), pp. 9-25.

[16]Pope John XXIII, Populorum Progressio as quoted in the Bishops' Letter, En Los Días de La Guerra, July 7, 1979.

[17] Conferencia Episcopal de Nicaragua a los hombres de buena voluntad, August 3, 1978.

[18]En Los Días de Guerra, July 7, 1979.

[19]Ibid.

[20] Conferencia Episcopal de Nicaragua a los hombres de buena voluntad, August 3, 1978.

[21]Interview with Minister of Housing and Human Affairs, Miguel Ernesto Vigil. These facts were confirmed in an interview with Enrique Alvarez Montalban, member of the Editorial Board of La Prensa, who accompanied Obando during these negotiations. In an interesting perspective on these negotiations, Somoza's newspaper, Novedades, referred to these meetings in Caracas and described the participants as "elements that move inside the continental communist

105

network against the leader of Nicaragua." <u>Novedades</u>, July 15, 1979, p. 15.

[22]This reference to Sandino comes from a 1980 speech of Tomás Borge, Minister of the Interior.

[23]This letter was not to be found at the Centro Antonio Valdivieso, Central American Historical Institute, the archives of the Episcopate, or of Radio Católica or in <u>La</u> <u>Prensa</u>.

[24]One Sandinist, in speaking of the letter, said, "just as the church has its dogmatists we have ours too."

[25]According to several charismatic critics, the government tried to change the Catholic meaning of Christmas and they could not do it; to do so they would "have to destroy Christianity and create another religion." Interview with Enrique A. Montalban, July 13, 1982.

[26] <u>El</u> <u>Nuevo</u> <u>Diario</u>, November 26, 1980, p. 10.

[27]<u>La</u> <u>Barricada</u> <u>Internacional</u>, December 30, 1982, p. 3.

[28]The "<u>purísima</u>" is the festival to Mary which takes place during the Christmas celebration and lasts for 12 days. During this time, Catholic homes construct altars to Mary, and children visit homes in their neighborhood and receive candies, fruits, or gifts from each house they visit. The holiday begins with a traditional "<u>gritería</u>" (a call and a response in honor of the Immaculate Conception of Mary).

[29]<u>La</u> <u>Prensa</u>, November 29, 1980, p. 5.

[30]<u>La</u> <u>Prensa</u>, November 29, 1980, p. 2.

[31]Ibid.

[32]<u>Official</u> <u>Communiqué</u> <u>of</u> <u>the</u> <u>National</u> <u>Directorate</u> <u>Concerning</u> <u>Religion</u>, p. 6.

[33]Ibid.

[34]The bishops said: "Our process will be something creative, original, profoundly national and not imitative. Because, like the majority of Nicaraguans what we want is a process toward a society which is authentically Nicaraguan, not capitalist, nor dependent nor totalitarian." <u>Compromiso</u> <u>Cristiano</u>

Para Una Nicaragua Nueva, November 17, 1979, n.p., p. 9.

[35]Compromiso Cristiano Para Una Nicaragua Nueva, November 17, 1979, pp. 8-9.

[36]At the time this controversy began (May 1980) Father Parrales was still the Minister of Welfare and Father Argüello was not yet the ACLEN delegate to the Council of State. However, the basic issues have remained the same.

[37]Comunicado Pastoral de 13 de Mayo de 1980, Sacerdotes en el Gobierno Nicaragüense: Poder o Servicio? (San José, Costa Rica: DEI, n.d.), p. 7.

[38]The direct quotation within the bishops' communiqué is from the Final Document of the Puebla Conference, No. 919.

[39]Comunicado de La Conferencia Episcopal de Nicaragua, Sacerdotes en el Gobierno Nicaragüense: Poder o Servicio? (San José, Costa Rica: DEI, n.d.), p. 9.

[40]Pax Christi International Human Rights Reports of the Mission: Nicaragua (Antwerpen, Belgium: Omega Books, 1981), p. 98.

[41]"The Ministerial Priesthood," Part Two, No. 2 of the 1971 Synod of Bishops in Eagleson, John, and Scharper, Philip, eds., Puebla and Beyond (Maryknoll, N.Y.: Orbis Books, 1979), p. 197.

[42]"Final Document" (526, 527) in Eagleson, John and Scharper, Philip, eds., Puebla and Beyond (Maryknoll, N.Y.: Orbis Books, 1979), pp. 196-197.

[43] Communiqué of the Priests Who Work in Government, May 20, 1980.

[44]"Primera Respuesta de Sacerdotes," June 8, 1981 in Sacerdotes en el Gobierno Nicaragüense: Poder o Servicio? (San José, Costa Rica: DEI), p. 12.

[45]Official Communiqué Concerning Religion of the FSLN, p. 9.

[46]After the April 1980 meeting, Obando was quoted as saying, "The church believes that an atheistic ideology cannot be the instrument that promotes social justice, because it deprives man of his spiritual inheritance. The Church has a right to be able to

maintain its own institutions for the normal fulfill-
ment of its specific mission." La Prensa, May 24,
1980.

[47] El Nuevo Diario, July 17, 1981, in Nicaragua
Noticias, no. 34.

[48] Declaration of the Special Mission that went to
the Vatican, October 20, 1980.

[49] La Barricada, July 16, 1981, p. 1.

[50] Statement of the Episcopal Conference of
Nicaragua, February 18, 1982.

[51] The allegations of brutality including mass
murders and people buried alive were rejected by the
Americas Watch Report of May 1982 and the Amnesty
International briefing that December.

[52] According to Vigil, he and Schlaefer met on
Monday, February 15, and discussed the Misquito
problem during the morning. On February 17, Vigil
travelled to the Misquito areas. On his return trip,
he read the bishops' letter in the papers. Vigil
summarized his response to the letter as one of
betrayal. Interview, July 2, 1982, with Housing
Minister Miguel Ernesto Vigil.

[53] According to Vigil, Schlaefer commented that
the Misquito response to a suggested relocation was to
resist because "the bones of our fathers are buried
here." Interview, M.E. Vigil.

[54] Interview, Sixto Ulloa, Director of Public
Relations, CEPAD, June 20, 1982.

[55] But the archbishop refused to specify who the
informants were and how they obtained their information. Interview, July 10, 1982.

[56] Interview, July 10, 1982.

[57] See the coverage in El Nuevo Diario, August 24,
1982. Apparently, Horacio Ruíz, of La Prensa first
alleged that Bishop Schlaefer had been imprisoned.
When Ruíz was questioned he stated that the archbishop
had given him this information. See El Nuevo Diario,
August 20, 1982.

[58] La Prensa, June 29, 1982, p. 1.

[59] La Prensa, July 31, 1982.

[60]No printed copy of this sermon could be found in Managua, but it was clear that it had been delivered.

[61]"The Revolution Fights Against the Theology of Death," _Informes_ (Managua, Nicaragua: CAV, June 14, 1982), n.p.

[62]Ibid.

[63]"Documento de la Conferencia Episcopal de Nicaragua," October 17, 1980, _Nicaragua: La Hora de los Desafíos_ (Lima, Perú: Centro de Estudios y Publicaciones, 1981), p. 121.

[64]Ibid., p. 114.

[65]_Jesucristo y La Unidad de su Iglesia en Nicaragua_ (Managua, Nicaragua: Editorial Unión, 1980), p. 3.

[66]Ibid.

[67]Archbishop Obando maintained in response to my questions that 1) the Episcopal Conference did not meet regularly but only when the need arose, and 2) all the bishops had to agree on the contents of any letter before it could be issued in the name of the Episcopal Conference. Interview, July 10, 1982.

[68]_Envío_, January 26, 1981. (Managua, Nicaragua: Instituto Histórico Centro Americano), n.p.

[69]_El Nuevo Diario_, May 20, 1980.

[70]_Barricada_, October 3, 1982.

[71]_Ibid_.

[72]Leamos' La carta del Papa, Episcopal Conference, June 29, 1982.

[73]_Latin American Weekly Report_, 83-35, September 9, 1983, p. 11.

[74]In conversations with me, revolutionary Christians indicated that their reaction to being labelled a parallel church ranged from confusion to insult and to resentment.

[75]"Open Letter to Pope John Paul II from Catholics in Nicaragua," August 15, 1982, in _Church and Revolution in Nicaragua_, _Special Report Central_

America Update (Toronto, Canada: LAWG, November 1982), pp. 9-12.

[76] *New York Times*, March 6, 1983, p. 14.

[77] "Arzobispo Retira Licencia al P. Oliva," *Amanecer*, Mayo-Junio, 1983, p. 3.

[78] Sagrada Congregación Para el Clero, Rome, July 14, 1983. Recently, CONFER, the Nicaraguan Association of Religious, has received a similar request from Rome to revise its statutes.

[79] In interviews conducted with them, priests who were members of ACLEN and other concerned Christians indicated that the possibility for dialogue with the Episcopal Conference seemed to be nil.

[80] "Mártires de la iglesia y de la Revolución" in *Amanecer*, Julio-Agosto, 1983, pp. 14, 15. Also *el Tayacán*, August 1983, and interviews with several priests from Managua and Estelí, who prefer to remain anonymous.

[81] The bishops stated: "This bill is highly politicized in its basic points, has a partisan character and follows the general lines of all totalitarian type legislation." See "General Considerations on Military Service," August 29, 1983, *La Prensa*, September 1, 1983.

[82] *El Nuevo Diario*, September 6, 1983. The rumor in Managua, as of early September, was that the vote among the bishops was 4 in favor of the communiqué, 3 opposed. The two remaining bishops were not present at the meeting but were opposed. As of this writing I was not able to confirm this.

[83] On the latter point, Sr. Núñez was quite clear that the bloc leaders were not authorized to do this, as it was clearly premature.

[84] "Peregrinación", *Barricada Internacional*, no. 85, October 17, 1983.

[85] In early November, two foreign priests were expelled from Nicaragua. The government claimed that they were encouraging the people not to participate in the draft. *New York Times*, Nov. 7, 1983.

[86] *The Church in Nicaragua* (Huntington, Indiana: Our Sunday Visitor, November 7, 1982).

PART 2 NOTES[*]

[1]Marx, K., <u>Prologue</u> to <u>The</u> <u>Critique</u> <u>of</u> <u>Political</u> <u>Economy</u>, (Mexico: Pasado y Presente, 1980).
Lenin, <u>What</u> <u>Is</u> <u>to</u> <u>Be</u> <u>Done</u>?, (Moscow: Progress, 1969).

[2]Althusser, L., <u>Ideology</u> <u>and</u> <u>Ideological</u> <u>Apparatus</u> <u>of</u> <u>the</u> <u>State</u>., (Buenos Aires: Nueva Vision, 1975).

[3]Portantiero, J. C., <u>The</u> <u>Uses</u> <u>of</u> <u>Gramsci</u>, (Mexico: 1981).

[4]Silva, L., <u>The</u> <u>Theory</u> <u>and</u> <u>Practice</u> <u>of</u> <u>Ideology</u>, (Mexico: Nuevo Tiempo, 1974).

[5]Houtart, F., "La Religíon y La Reproducíon Capitalista", (Managua: ANICS, Sept. 1982).

[6]Maduro, O., <u>Religion</u> <u>and</u> <u>Social</u> <u>Conflict</u>, (Mexico: Center for Theological Reflection, 1980).

[7]Gutiérrez, G., <u>The</u> <u>Theology</u> <u>of</u> <u>Liberation</u>, (Salamanca: Sígueme, 1980).

[8]National Directorate of the F.S.L.N., <u>Official</u> <u>Communiqué</u> <u>Concerning</u> <u>Religion</u>, October 10, 1980.

[9]Maier, E., <u>Nicaragua</u>, <u>La</u> <u>Mujer</u> <u>en</u> <u>la</u> <u>Revolución</u>, (Mexico Cultura Popular, 1980).
Randall, M., <u>Estamos</u> <u>Despiertas</u>, (Mexico, Siglo XXI, 1980).

---

*Editor's note: Originally presented to an academic audience in NIcaragua, the paper from which this section was translated sometimes lacks the type of citation which would be useful to a foreign readership less familiar with the material. In some cases the editor and translator have succeeded in supplying such citations. In other cases, regrettably, we have not been able to provide this service. The overall importance of this paper in providing an informed alternative point of view, however, justifies its publication without further delay. For background information about both authors and their perspectives, see the introduction.

[10] AMPRONAC, "Programa", citado en Maier, op. cit.

[11] Ramírez-Horton, S.E., "Women in the Revolution," in Walker, T., Nicaragua in Revolution, (New York: Praeger, 1982).

[12] Frente Patriótico Nacional, "Documento sobre la problemática actual," (Managua: 1978).

[13] Castilla, M. de, Educacíon y lucha de clases en Nicaragua, (Managua: UCA, 1980).
Ministerio de Educacíon, La Educacíon en el primer año de la Revolución Popular Sandinista, (Managua: 1980).
Arrien, J. y otros, Educacíon y Dependencia, (Managua: INPRHU, 1977).

[14] Stuart, D., La Crisis de la Escuela en la Sociedad Capitalista, (Managua: Farach, 1976).

[15] Wheelock, J., Imperialismo y Dictadura, (Mexico: Siglo XXI, 1979).

[16] Castilla, M. de, "La Educación como Poder," (Congreso: ANICS, 1981).

[17] Arce, B., "Por una Cultura Revolucionaria," Barricada, February 22, 1980.

[18] Castilla, M. de, Pedagogía del Neocolonialismo, (Managua: UCA, 1979).

[19] Ramírez, S., "Balcanes y Volcanes," en Centroamérica Hoy, (Mexico: Siglo XXI, 1973).

[20] Chávez, A.L., entrevista en Plural, No. 106, (Mexico: Julio, 1980).

[21] Stuart, op. cit.

[22] Dorfman, A. y otros, Imperialismo y Medios Masivos de Comunicación, (Mexico: Quinto Sol).

[23] Ramírez, S., op. cit.

[24] Wheelock, Imperialismo, op. cit.

[25] Alvarado, E., Investigación sobre el sistema televisivo, (Managua: UCA, 1977).

[26] Mattelard, en Imperialismo, op. cit.

112

[27]Dorfman, A., _Para leer el Pato Donald_, (Mexico: Siglo XXI, 1975).

[28]Ramírez, S., op. cit.

[29]Ibid.

[30]Lacayo, R., "Anotaciones sobre la cultura en la revolución," _Ventana_.

[31]Ramírez, S., op. cit.

[32]Nichols, J., "The News Media in the Nicaraguan Revolution," in Walker, op. cit.

[33]Ibid.

[34]Puiggros A., _Imperialismo y educación en América Latina_, (México: Nueva Imagen, 1980).

[35]Dussel, E., _Historia de la Iglesia en América Latina_, (Barcelona: Nova Terra, 1971).

[36]Esguevar A., "La religión entre los indígenas nicaragüenses", (Managua: UCA, 1980).

[37]Arellano, J., _Breve historia de la iglesia en Nicaragua_, (Managua: 1980).

[38]Ibid.

[39]Ciera, _La Mosquita en la Revolución_, (Managua: 1981).

[40]Torres, J., "La iglesia evangélica protestante," en _Apuntes para una Teología Nicaragüense_, (Costa Rica: DEI, 1981).

[41]Ibid.

[42]Ortega, H., _50 años de lucha sandinista_, (Managua: Depep, 1980).

[43]Argüello, A., _Fé Cristiana y Revolución Sandinista_, (IHCA-Mec, 1980).
Lopéz J., y otros, _La caída del somocismo y la lucha sandinista en Nicaragua_, (Costa Rica: Educa, 1979).

[44]Junta de Gobierno de Reconstrucción Nacional, "La revolución a tres años del triunfo," (Managua: 1982).

113

[45]JGRN, "Principios y políticas del Gobierno de Reconstrucción Nacional," (Managua: 1982).

[46]Cardenal, E., Diálogo en Asamblea de ASTC, Feb. 1980.

[47]Lacayo, op. cit.

[48]Núñez, C., Charla en Asamblea de ASTC, Marzo, 1982.

[49]Nichols, op. cit.

[50]UNAN, Apuntes para el curso sobre la problemática actual, (Managua: 1980).

[51]Landis, F., "Estudio de Chile, Jamaica y Nicaragua: la CIA opera así en los medios de comunicación," NUEVO DIARIO, 1-6/2/80.
Borge, T., "La contrarevolución y los medios de comunicación," Conferencia en la Casa del Periodista, 26/1/82.
Gargurevich, J., A golpe de titular, la CIA y el periodismo en América Latina, (Lima: 1981).
Nuevo Diario, March, 1982.

[52]Borge, T., Diálogo, Asamblea de AMNLAE, Oct. 1982.

[53]Meier, op. cit.

[54]Ramírez, S., El Pensamiento Vivo de Sandino, (Managua: Nueva Nicaragua, 1981).

[55]Fonseca, C., Bajo la bandera del sandinismo, (Managua, Depep, 1980).

[56]Borge, T., "Las cualidades del militante sandinista," (Managua: Depep, 1980).

[57]National Directorate of the F.S.L.N., Official Communiqué Concerning Religion, (October, 1980).

[58]Torres, A. y otros, "La lucha ideológica en el campo religioso y su significado político," ponencia, Cong. ANICS.

[59]Pax Christi, "Informe de visita a Nicaragua," Managua, Inst. -- Juan XXIII, 82.

[60]Agee, P., "Maniobras de la CIA en Nicaragua," Poder Sandinista, Nov., 1981.

[61] Conferencia Episcopal de Nicaragua, Comunicado, 16/5/80.

[62] Torres, op. cit., II-21.

[63] Conferencia Episcopal, Carta del 17/10 1980.

[64] La Prensa, Aug. 31, 1980, M. Obando.

[65] La Prensa, Sept. 7, 1980, M. Obando.

[66] La Prensa, Dec. 20, 1980.

[67] La Prensa, Feb. 15, 1981.

[68] Torres, op. cit., II-19.

[69] Nuevo Diario, March 12, 1981.

[70] Nuevo Diario, March 4, 1982.

[71] La Prensa, Jan. 22, 1981.

[72] Pax Christi, op. cit., p. 54.

[73] Tesis: Iglesia Adventista del 70, "Día en un Mundo Progresista" (Managua: Sept., 1982).

[74] Folleto, "Cuando Dios Habla," no. 11 y Serie, "Cristo Vicar", No. 7.

[75] Nuevo Diario, Jan., 1982.

[76] La Prensa, Feb. 2, 1982.

[77] La Prensa, Oct. 12, 1981.

[78] Landis, op. cit.; Gargurevich, op. cit.; Serra, op. cit.

[79] La Prensa, May 9, 1981, p. 1.

[80] La Prensa, January 31, 1982.

[81] Nuevo Diario, Jan. 23, 1982.

[82] La Prensa, February 21, 1982.

[83] La Prensa, May 3, 1982.

[84] La Prensa, May 10, 1982.

[85] La Prensa, Nov. 30, 1980, and Jan. 22, 1981.

[86] Conferencia Episcopal, Carta del 22/10/1980.

[87] Gil, R. L., *Informes* CAV, No. 7 (Managua: Centro Valdivieso, Oct. 1981).

[88] Centro Valdivieso, *Amanecer No. 13*, Oct. 1982.

[89] Gil, op. cit.

[90] Agee, P., "Conferencia Sobre la Actuación de la CIA en las Instituciones religiosas," CAV. Oct. 16, 1981.

[91] Plan de Santa Fé, *Soberanía*, Tribunal Antimperialista, Oct. 19, 1981 (No. 1).

[92] Girardi, G., Conversatorio de ANICS, op. cit.

[93] Maduro, O., *Religión y Conflicto.*, op. cit.

LIST OF ABBREVIATIONS AND ORGANIZATIONS

ACLEN - Nicaraguan Council of Clergy
APM - Association of Journalists of Nicaragua
ATC - Association of Rural Workers
CDS - Sandinist Defense Committee
CEB - Basic Christian Community
CELAM - Episcopal Conference of Latin America
CEN - Episcopal Conference of Nicaragua
CEPA - Center for Aquarian Education and Promotion
CEPAD - Protestant Development Committee
CIA - United States Central Intelligence Agency
CNA - National Literacy Crusade
CONFER - Nicaraguan Association of Religions
COPPPAL - Permanent Conference of Political Parties of
      Latin America
COSEP - High Council of Private Industry
FAO - Broad Opposition Front
FPN - National Patriotic Front
FSLN - Frente Sandinista De Liberacion Nacional GRN -
Government of National Reconstruction
INCAE - Central American Institute of Business
      Administration
JGRN - Council of the Government of National
      Reconstruction
MCM - Means of Mass Communication
MEP - Ministry of Popular Education
MESCATE -
MOB - Monsignor Obando y Bravo
MPU - United People's Movement
RPS - Popular Sandinista Revolution
UCA - Central American University
UDEL - Democratic Liberation Union
UNAG - Union of [small] Cattlemen and Ranchers
UPN - Journalists Union of Nicaragua

THE AUTHORS

LAURA NUZZI O'SHAUGHNESSY is Associate Professor of Government at Saint Lawrence University, Canton, NY. She is the author of articles and chapters on Mexico, El Salvador, Honduras and Nicaragua.

Professor O'Shaughnessy received her B.A. from Queens College of the City University of New York (1966) and her M.A. and Ph.D. (1977) degrees from Indiana University. She was a member of Mutuality in Mission, an interdenominational lay mission team which travelled to Central America in 1981 to observe the role of the churches in that region. Since then, she has returned to Nicaragua various times on research trips.

LUIS HECTOR SERRA, an Argentine, is a Professor of Sociology at the Central American University in Managua. Since 1979, he has resided in Nicaragua where he has worked in the Literacy Crusade, with the Christian revolutionary movement, and with peasant popular education. In that respect, he presently works as an advisor to the National Union of Farmers and Cattlemen (UNAG), the popular organization of small and medium landholders.

Professor Serra is a graduate in law and history from the National University of Buenos Aires. He also holds M.A. degrees in International Affairs and Political Science from Ohio University. His columns on Church-State relations and other matters, have appeared frequently in Managua's daily, Nuevo Diario. His recent works include "Educación en América Latina" (1983) and shorter pieces on grassroots mobilization in Nicaragua.

ISBN Prefix 0-89680-

Africa Series

16. Weisfelder, Richard F. THE BASOTHO MONARCHY: A Spent Force or
     Dynamic Political Factor? 1972. 106 pp.
     043-0   (82-91676) $ 7.00*

19. Huntsberger, Paul E., compiler. HIGHLAND MOSAIC: A
     Critical Anthology of Ethiopian Literature in English.
     1973. 122 pp.
     052-0   (82-91700) $ 7.00*

21. Silberfein, Marilyn. CONSTRAINTS ON THE EXPANSION OF
     COMMERICAL AGRICULTURE: Iringa District, Tanzania.
     1974. 51 pp.
     054-7   (82-91726) $ 4.50*

22. Pieterse, Cosmo. ECHO AND CHORUSES: "Ballad of the Cells"
     and Selected Shorter Poems. 1974. 66 pp.
     055-5   (82-91734) $ 5.00*

23. Thom, Derrick J. THE NIGER-NIGERIA BOUNDARY: A
     Study of Ethnic Frontiers and a Colonial Boundary.
     1975. 50 pp.
     056-3   (82-91742) $ 4.75*

24. Baum, Edward compiler. A COMPREHENSIVE PERIODICAL BIBLIO-
     GRAPHY OF NIGERIA, 1960-1970. 1975. 250 pp.
     057-1   (82-91759) $13.00*

25. Kirchherr, Eugene C. ABYSSINIA TO ZIMBABWE: A Guide to the
     Political Units of Africa in the Period 1947-1978. 1979,
     3rd Ed. 80 pp.
     100-4   (82-91908) $ 8.00*

27. Fadiman, Jeffrey A. MOUNTAIN WARRIORS: The Pre-Colonial
     Meru of Mt. Kenya. 1976. 82 pp.
     060-1   (82-91783) $ 4.75*

32. Wright, Donald R. THE EARLY HISTORY OF THE NIUMI: Settle-
     ment and Foundation of a Mandinka State on the Gambia River.
     1977. 122 pp.
     064-4   (82-91833) $ 8.00*

36. Fadiman, Jeffrey A. THE MOMENT OF CONQUEST: Meru, Kenya,
     1907. 1979. 70 pp.
     081-4   (82-91874) $ 5.50*

37. Wright, Donald R. ORAL TRADITIONS FROM THE GAMBIA: Volume
     I, Mandinka Griots. 1979. 176 pp.
     083-0   (82-91882) $12.00*

38. Wright, Donald R.   ORAL TRADITIONS FROM THE GAMBIA: Volume
    II, Family Elders.   1980.   200 pp.
    084-9   (82-91890) $15.00*

39. Reining, Priscilla.   CHALLENGING DESERTIFICATION IN WEST
    AFRICA: Insights from Landsat into Carrying Capacity,
    Cultivation and Settlement Site Identification in Upper
    Volta and Niger.   1979.   180 pp., illus.
    102-0   (82-91916) $12.00*

41. Lindfors, Bernth.   MAZUNGUMZO: Interviews with East African
    Writers, Publishers, Editors, and Scholars.   1981.   179 pp.
    108-X   (82-91932) $13.00*

42. Spear, Thomas J.   TRADITIONS OF ORIGIN AND THEIR INTERPRET-
    ATION: The Mijikenda of Kenya.   1982.   xii, 163 pp.
    109-8   (82-91940) $13.50*

43. Harik, Elsa M. and Donald G. Schilling.   THE POLITICS OF
    EDUCATION IN COLONIAL ALGERIA AND KENYA.   1984.   102 pp.
    117-9   (82-91957) $11.50*

44. Smith, Daniel R.   THE INFLUENCE OF THE FABIAN COLONIAL
    BUREAU ON THE INDEPENDENCE MOVEMENT IN TANGANYIKA.   1985.
    x, 98 pp.
    125-X   (82-91965) $ 9.00*

45. Keto, C. Tsehloane.   AMERICAN-SOUTH AFRICAN RELATIONS 1784-
    1980:   Review and Select Bibliography.   1985.   c. 174 pp.
    128-4   (82-91973) $11.00*

46. Burness, Don, and Mary-Lou Burness, ed.   WANASEMA:
    Conversations with African Writers.   1985.   c. 108 pp.
    129-2   (82-91981) $ 9.00*

47. Switzer, Les.   MEDIA AND DEPENDENCY IN SOUTH AFRICA: A Case
    Study of the Press and the Ciskei "Homeland".   1985.
    c. 97 pp.
    130-6   (82-91999) $ 9.00*

Latin America Series

1. Frei M., Eduardo.   THE MANDATE OF HISTORY AND CHILE'S FUTURE.
   Tr. by Miguel d'Escoto.   Intro. by Thomas Walker.   1977.
   79 pp.
   066-0   (82-92526) $ 8.00*

2. Irish, Donald P., ed. MULTINATIONAL CORPORATIONS IN LATIN
   AMERICA: Private Rights--Public Responsibilities.   1978.
   135 pp.
   067-9   (82-92534) $ 9.00*

4. Martz, Mary Jeanne Reid. THE CENTRAL AMERICAN SOCCER WAR:
    Historical Patterns and Internal Dynamics of OAS Settlement
    Procedures. 1979. 118 pp.
    077-6   (82-92559) $ 8.00*

5. Wiarda, Howard J. CRITICAL ELECTIONS AND CRITICAL COUPS:
    State, Society, and the Military in the Processes of Latin
    American Development. 1979. 83 pp.
    082-2   (82-92567) $ 7.00*

6. Dietz, Henry A. and Richard Moore. POLITICAL PARTICIPATION
    IN A NON-ELECTORAL SETTING: The Urban Poor in Lima, Peru.
    1979. viii, 102 pp.
    085-7   (82-92575) $ 9.00*

7. Hopgood, James F. SETTLERS OF BAJAVISTA: Social and
    Economic Adaptation in a Mexican Squatter Settlement. 1979.
    xii, 145 pp.
    101-2   (82-92583) $11.00*

8. Clayton, Lawrence A. CAULKERS AND CARPENTERS IN A NEW WORLD:
    The Shipyards of Colonial Guayaquil. 1980. 189 pp., illus.
    103-9   (82-92591) $15.00*

9. Tata, Robert J. STRUCTURAL CHANGES IN PUERTO RICO'S ECONOMY:
    1947-1976. 1981. xiv, 104 pp.
    107-1   (82-92609) $11.75*

10. McCreery, David. DEVELOPMENT AND THE STATE IN REFORMA
    GUATEMALA, 1871-1885. 1983. viii, 120 pp.
    113-6   (82-92617) $ 8.50*

Southeast Asia Series

31. Nash, Manning. PEASANT CITIZENS: Politics, Religion, and
    Modernization in Kelantan, Malaysia. 1974. 181 pp.
    018-0   (82-90322) $12.00*

44. Collier, William L., et al. INCOME, EMPLOYMENT AND FOOD
    SYSTEMS IN JAVANESE COASTAL VILLAGES. 1977. 160 pp.
    031-8   (82-90454) $10.00*

47. Wessing, Robert. COSMOLOGY AND SOCIAL BEHAVIOR IN A WEST
    JAVANESE SETTLEMENT. 1978. 200 pp.
    072-5   (82-90488) $12.00*

48. Willer, Thomas F., ed. SOUTHEAST ASIAN REFERENCES IN THE
    BRITISH PARLIAMENTARY PAPERS, 1801-1972/73: An Index.
    1977. 110 pp.
    033-4   (82-90496) $ 8.50*

50. Echauz, Robustiano. SKETCHES OF THE ISLAND OF NEGROS.
    1978. 174 pp.
    070-9   (82-90512) $10.00*

51. Kramrich, Ronald L. MAYORS AND MANAGERS IN THAILAND: The
    Struggle for Political Life in Administrative Settings.
    1978. 139 pp.
    073-3   (82-90520) $ 9.00*

52. Davis, Gloria, ed. WHAT IS MODERN INDONESIAN CULTURE? 1978.
    300 pp.
    075-X   (82-90538) $18.00*

54. Ayal, Eliezar B., ed. THE STUDY OF THAILAND: Analyses of
    Knowledge, Approaches, and Prospects in Anthropology, Art
    History, Economics, History and Political Science. 1979.
    257 pp.
    079-2   (82-90553) $13.50*

56. Duiker, William J. VIETNAM SINCE THE FALL OF SAIGON.
    Second Edition, Revised and Enlarged. 1985. c. 300 pp.
    133-0   (82-90744) $12.00*

57. Siregar, Susan Rodgers. ADAT, ISLAM, AND CHRISTIANITY IN A
    BATAK HOMELAND. 1981. 108 pp.
    110-1   (82-90587) $10.00*

58. Van Esterik, Penny. COGNITION AND DESIGN PRODUCTION IN BAN
    CHIANG POTTERY. 1981. 90 pp.
    078-4   (82-90595) $12.00*

59. Foster, Brian L. COMMERCE AND ETHNIC DIFFERENCES: The Case
    of the Mons in Thailand. 1982. x, 93 pp.
    112-8   (82-90603) $10.00*

60. Frederick, William H. and John H. McGlynn. REFLECTIONS ON
    REBELLION: Stories from the Indonesian Upheavals of 1948
    and 1965. 1983. vi, 168 pp.
    111-X   (82-90611) $ 9.00*

61. Cady, John F. CONTACTS WITH BURMA, 1935-1949: A Personal
    Account. 1983. x, 117 pp.
    114-4   (82-90629) $ 9.00*

62. Kipp, Rita Smith and Richard D. Kipp, eds. BEYOND SAMOSIR:
    Recent Studies of the Batak Peoples of Sumatra. 1983.
    viii, 155 pp.
    115-2   (82-90637) $ 9.00*

63. Carstens, Sharon, ed. CULTURAL IDENTITY IN NORTHERN
    PENINSULAR MALAYSIA. 1985. c. 109 pp.
    116-0   (62-90645)   forthcoming $ 9.00*

64. Dardjowidjojo, Soenjono. VOCABULARY BUILDING IN INDONESIAN:
    An Advanced Reader. 1984. xviii, 256 pp.
    118-7   (82-90652) $18.00*

65. Errington, J. Joseph. LANGUAGE AND SOCIAL CHANGE IN JAVA:
    Linguistic Reflexes of Modernization in a Traditional Royal
    Polity. 1985. xiv, 198 pp.
    120-9   (82-90660) $12.00*

66. Binh, Tran Tu. THE RED EARTH: A Vietnamese Memoir of Life
    on a Colonial Rubber Plantation. Tr. by John Spragens.
    Ed. by David Marr. 1985. xii, 98 pp.
    119-5   (82-90678) $ 9.00*

67. Pane, Armijn. SHACKLES. Tr. by John McGlynn. Intro. by
    William H. Frederick. 1985. xvi, 108 pp.
    122-5   (82-90686) $ 9.00*

68. Syukri, Ibrahim. HISTORY OF THE MALAY KINGDOM OF PATANI.
    Tr. by Conner Bailey and John N. Miksic. 1985. xx, 98 pp.
    123-3   (82-90694) $10.50*

69. Keeler, Ward. JAVANESE: A Cultural Approach. 1984.
    xxxvi, 523 pp.
    121-7   (82-90702) $18.00*

70. Wilson, Constance M. and Lucien M. Hanks. BURMA-THAILAND
    FRONTIER OVER SIXTEEN DECADES: Three Descriptive Documents.
    1985. x, 128 pp.
    124-1   (82-90710) $10.50*

71. Thomas, Lynn L. and Franz von Benda-Beckmann, eds. CHANGE
    AND CONTINUITY IN MINANGKABAU: Local, Regional, and
    Historical Perspectives on West Sumatra. 1985. c. 360 pp.
    127-6   (82-90728)   forthcoming $14.00*

72. Reid, Anthony and Oki Akira, eds. THE JAPANESE EXPERIENCE
    IN INDONESIA: Selected Memoirs of 1942-1945. 1985.
    c. 450 pp., 20 illus.
    132-2   (82-90736)   forthcoming $18.00*

ORDERING INFORMATION

        Orders for titles in the Monographs in International Studies
series should be placed through the Ohio University Press/Scott
Quadrangle/Athens, Ohio, 45701-2979. Individuals must remit
prepayment via check, VISA, MasterCard, CHOICE, or American
Express. Individuals ordering from outside of the U.S. please
remit in U.S. funds by either International Money Order or check
drawn on a U.S. bank. Residents of Ohio and Missouri please add
sales tax. Postage and handling is $2.00 for the first book and
$.50 for each additional book. Prices and availability are
subject to change without notice.